Mike McGrath

GO
Programming

In easy steps is an imprint of In Easy Steps Limited
16 Hamilton Terrace · Holly Walk · Leamington Spa
Warwickshire · United Kingdom · CV32 4LY
www.ineasysteps.com

Notice of Liability
Every effort has been made to ensure that this book contains accurate
and current information. However, In Easy Steps Limited and the
author shall not be liable for any loss or damage suffered by readers
as a result of any information contained herein.

Trademarks
All trademarks are acknowledged as belonging to their respective
companies.

In Easy Steps Limited supports The Forest Stewardship Council (FSC),
the leading international forest certification organization. All our titles
that are printed on Greenpeace approved FSC certified paper carry the
FSC logo.

MIX
Paper from
responsible sources
FSC® C020837

Printed and bound in the United Kingdom

ISBN 978-1-84078-919-5

Contents

How to Use This Book

The examples in this book demonstrate features of the Go programming language ("golang"), and the screenshots illustrate the actual results produced by the listed code examples. Certain colorization conventions are used to clarify the code listed in the steps...

Program code is colored black but keywords and built-in functions of the Go language are colored blue, literal text and numeric values are red, and code comments are green, like this:

```go
package main
import "fmt"
    main( ) {

        // My First Go Program.
        fmt.Println( "Hello World!" )
}
```

During setup of Go, you will select a "GOPATH" location on your computer in which to create programs. Each program will be created within a uniquely named folder in a GOPATH sub-directory named "src". To identify the source code for the example programs described in the steps, an icon and file path appears in the margin alongside the steps:

src/hello/main.go

Grab the Source Code

For convenience, the source code files from all examples featured in this book are available in a single ZIP archive. You can obtain this archive by following these easy steps:

1. Browse to **www.ineasysteps.com** then navigate to Free Resources and choose the Downloads section

2. Next, find GO Programming in easy steps in the list, then click on the hyperlink entitled All Code Examples to download the ZIP archive file

3. Now, extract the archive contents to the GOPATH/**src** sub-directory on your computer

If you don't achieve the result illustrated in any example, simply compare your code to that in the original example files you have downloaded to discover where you went wrong.

1 Get Started

Meet the Go Language

The Go gopher – the iconic mascot of the Go programming language.

Go is a free open-source programming language created at Google by Robert Griesemer, Rob Pike, and Ken Thompson – best known for development of the Unix operating system. Google released version 1.0 of the Go language ("golang") in March 2012, since when it has gained widespread popularity.

Go programs are written in plain text, then compiled into machine code by the Go compiler to produce an executable binary version.

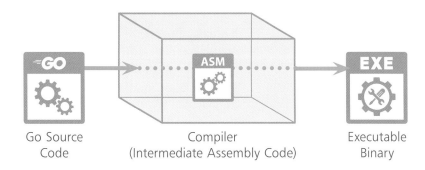

Go Source Code   Compiler (Intermediate Assembly Code)   Executable Binary

The aims of the Go programming language are to be expressive, fast, efficient, reliable, and simple to write. Some programming languages, such as C or C++, are fast and reliable but not simple. Conversely, other programming languages such as Java or Python are simple to write but not so efficient.

You can discover many more programming language books in the **In Easy Steps** series – including C, C++, C#, Java, and Python. Visit **www.ineasysteps.com** to find out more.

Hot tip

Go is similar to the C programming language in many ways, and is sometimes referred to as a "C-like language" or "C for the 21st century". But Go is much more than that, as it adopts good ideas from many other programming languages, yet avoids features that lead to complexity or unreliability.

Perhaps most importantly, Go introduces the ability to take advantage of multi-core CPU processing for concurrency using "goroutines" and "channels". This provides the potential for the computer to deal with several things at the same time.

Although the Go language does not have the class structures found in Object Oriented Programming (OOP) languages, such as C++ or Java, its features do provide some degree of encapsulation, inheritance, and polymorphism – the three cornerstones of OOP.

With so many programming languages to choose from, you may be wondering why you should choose to learn Go programming – so here are some of the advantages that Go offers:

Simple Syntax

The Go language is concise, like Python. It's as simple to write as Python but is more efficient, like C++. This enables you to write code that is easy to read and maintain.

Compiled Language

The Go source code is compiled to binary machine code that can be read directly by the computer, instead of being interpreted every time a program runs. This enables the Go programs you write to run faster than programs written for interpreted languages, like Python or PHP.

The Go Compiler

The Go compiler is fast and provides additional benefits, such as code optimization and error checking – it can detect unused variables in your code, missing imports that your code requires, and mistyped or invalid code. The Go compiler can also generate executable binaries for other operating systems. This enables you to compile your source code to run on multiple machines.

Concurrency

The Go language provides inherent support for concurrency with goroutines and channels. This enables you to write multi-threaded programs that could perform multiple tasks at the same time.

Garbage Collection

Automatic memory management is a key feature of the Go language. Its garbage collector runs concurrently with the program. This enables you to write program code without any concern for memory leakage.

Static Typing

Go is a statically typed language in which variables are explicitly declared to be of a particular fixed type. This enables errors to be caught early in the development process.

You may well recognize other advantages as you gain experience with the Go language, but right now it's time to get started...

Install the Go Tools

To get started with the Go programming language, you must first install the Go tools on your PC. These allow you to build, run, and test programs written in the Go language. The Go tools are supplied together with lots of standard packages of useful trusted code that you can import into your own programs. The Go language installers are available for Windows, macOS and Linux.

1 Open a web browser and visit **https://golang.org** then download the appropriate installer for your system

2 When the download has completed, run the installer to launch the "Go Programming Language Setup Wizard"

Hot tip

The Go installer for Windows should automatically add Go to your system path to make the Go tools available at a command prompt.

3 Click **Next** to continue, then accept the license terms

4 Accept the suggested **Destination Folder** (at **C:\Go** on Windows), then click **Install** to complete the installation

5 To test that the installation was successful, first open a Terminal window – on a Windows system press

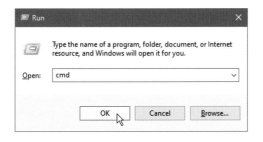

WinKey + **R** together, to open a "Run" dialog, then enter **cmd** to open a "Command Prompt" window

6 At the command prompt, type the command **go** then hit **Enter** to see a list of Go tool commands

The "WinKey" is the keyboard key labeled with the Windows logo.

```
C:\Users\mike_>go
Go is a tool for managing Go source code.

Usage:

        go <command> [arguments]

The commands are:

        bug         start a bug report
        build       compile packages and dependencies
        clean       remove object files and cached files
        doc         show documentation for package or symbol
        env         print Go environment information
        fix         update packages to use new APIs
        fmt         gofmt (reformat) package sources
        generate    generate Go files by processing source
        get         add dependencies to current module and install them
        install     compile and install packages and dependencies
        list        list packages or modules
        mod         module maintenance
        run         compile and run Go program
        test        test packages
        tool        run specified go tool
        version     print Go version
        vet         report likely mistakes in packages

Use "go help <command>" for more information about a command.

Additional help topics:

        buildmode      build modes
        c              calling between Go and C
        cache          build and test caching
        environment    environment variables
        filetype       file types
        go.mod         the go.mod file
        gopath         GOPATH environment variable
        gopath-get     legacy GOPATH go get
        goproxy        module proxy protocol
        importpath     import path syntax
        modules        modules, module versions, and more
        module-get     module-aware go get
        module-auth    module authentication using go.sum
        module-private module configuration for non-public modules
        packages       package lists and patterns
        testflag       testing flags
        testfunc       testing functions

Use "go help <topic>" for more information about that topic.
```

Although there are quite a few Go tools, you will mostly use only the **run** tool to compile and run your programs.

Create the Go Workspace

When you install Go, the installer sets a number of Go environment variables. For example, the directory (folder) location of the Go tools is stored in a **GOROOT** environment variable – by default, at **C:\Go** on a Windows PC, and at **/usr/local/go** on Linux and macOS.

The installer also sets a **GOPATH** environment variable for the location of your workspace. By default, this is a directory named "go" within your home directory. For example, on a Windows PC its path is **C:\Users***userName***\go**, on Linux systems its path is **/home/***userName***/go**, and on macOS it's at **/Users/***userName***/go** – but the installer doesn't actually create any directories.

To create the workspace, you can simply add a directory named "go" in your home directory. You must then add sub-directories named "bin", "pkg" and "src" within the workspace directory – all your Go programs can then be created inside the "src" directory.

It's useful to have a shortcut on your desktop that will open a command-line in this sub-directory to easily run your programs.

The **go\src** folder is where you will save the programs you write. The **go\bin** and **go\pkg** will be used later to store executable files and package archives.

1 On a Windows PC, open a Command Prompt window, as described on page 11, or open a Terminal window

2 Enter the command **go env GOPATH** to see the current expected workspace location

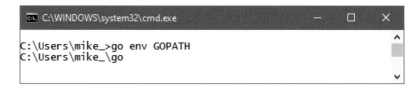

```
C:\WINDOWS\system32\cmd.exe                           —    □    ×

C:\Users\mike_>go env GOPATH
C:\Users\mike_\go
```

3 Next, issue a **mkdir** command to create the "go" workspace directory at the location specified by the **GOPATH** environment variable

The **mkdir** command name is simply short for "make directory".

```
C:\WINDOWS\system32\cmd.exe                           —    □    ×

C:\Users\mike_>mkdir go

C:\Users\mike_>_
```

4 Now, issue further **mkdir** commands to create the "bin", "pkg" and "src" sub-directories in the workspace directory

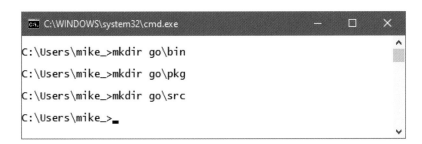

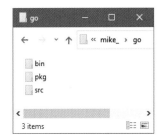

5 Right-click on a Windows desktop and select **New, Shortcut** to open a "Create Shortcut" dialog

6 Enter **cmd** as the location and click **Next**, then enter **Go Terminal** as the name and click **Finish** to create a shortcut icon on your desktop

7 Right-click on the shortcut icon and select the **Properties** item, to open its "Properties" dialog

8 Choose the **Shortcut** tab, then enter the location of your workspace directory

9 Click **Apply, OK** to close the dialog, then double-click the shortcut icon to open a command-line in your "src" folder

Hot tip

Go programs can be written in a plain text editor, such as Windows' Notepad app. It's useful to have a desktop shortcut that opens a text editor in your "src" directory folder. Repeat the steps on this page, but in Step 7 enter **notepad** as the location and **Go Editor** as the name, to create another useful desktop shortcut.

13

Write a Go Program

All Go programs start as plain text files that are later compiled into actual executable programs. This means that Go programs can be written in any plain text editor, such as the Windows' Notepad app or the Nano app on Linux.

Follow these steps to create a simple Go program that will output the traditional first program greeting:

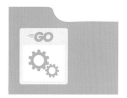

src/hello/main.go

1 Create a sub-directory named "hello" in your "src" folder

```
Go Terminal                                    —    □    ×

C:\Users\mike_\go\src>mkdir hello

C:\Users\mike_\go\src>_
```

2 Open a plain text editor, like Notepad, and type this code exactly as it is listed to begin a program
package main

3 Two lines below, insert this code exactly as it is listed
import "fmt"

4 Two further lines below, precisely add this code
func main( ) {

    fmt.Println("Hello World!")
}

Beware

Capital P and lowercase L in **fmt.Println**.

5 Save the file in the "hello" folder, and name it **main.go** – the complete program should now look exactly like this:

Don't forget

The arrangement of files within folders is important in Go. Each main file, and any related files, must be placed in a uniquely named folder to create a package – so here the package is named "hello".

```
main.go - Notepad                              —    □    ×
File  Edit  Format  View  Help
package main

import "fmt"

func main() {
        fmt.Println("Hello World!")
}
```

The separate parts of the program code on the opposite page can be examined individually to understand each part more clearly:

The Package Declaration

package main

The package type is declared following the **package** keyword. All Go program code is contained in packages. You may declare your own type for a package that will be a shared library, but you must declare the package "main" if you want the code to be compiled into an executable program.

The Import Declaration

import "fmt"

The keyword **import** is used to import one, or more, packages into this package to make their features available to this program. The package "fmt" comes from the Go standard library that is included in your Go installation. It provides the **fmt.Println( )** function that is used to output text in this program. Note that the package name must be enclosed in double quote characters. When importing multiple packages, the list of package names must be enclosed within parentheses and each name must appear on its own line, like this:

```
import (
    "fmt"
    "strings"
)
```

The Function Declaration

```
func main( ) {

        fmt.Println( "Hello World!" )
}
```

The function name follows the **func** keyword. It must be followed by parentheses and an **{** opening curly bracket on the same line. The function body contains statements that are the actual instructions to perform program tasks. The function body must end with a closing **}** curly bracket. Function names must be unique, but each Go program must have a function named "main" as this is the starting point of all Go programs.

The package <u>name</u> and package <u>type</u> are two separate items – here the package is named **hello**, but the type is **main**.

You can find the Go standard library packages in the "src" directory of your **GOROOT** directory location – for example, at **C:\Go\src**. Additionally, you can learn about each package from the official documentation at **https://golang.org/pkg** – an invaluable resource.

Run a Go Program

Go program code is compiled and executed using the Go tools. During program development, an error-free Go program can be compiled and run by the **go run** tool. This is useful, but if you want to create an executable binary file version that can be executed repeatedly and distributed, you can use the **go build** tool.

1 Open a Command Prompt or Terminal window in your Go "src" folder

2 Enter the command **go run hello** to run the program written on page 14 – it should output the greeting

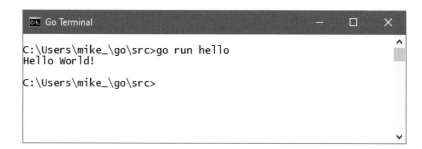

```
C:\Users\mike_\go\src>go run hello
Hello World!

C:\Users\mike_\go\src>
```

3 Next, enter the command **go build hello** to make an executable binary version of the program on page 14 – it should add an executable file in your "src" folder

4 Now, twice enter the command **hello** on Windows, or **./hello** on Linux or macOS – it should output the traditional greeting two times

On Windows systems the binary file is given the file extension **.exe**, so the file built here is **hello.exe**.

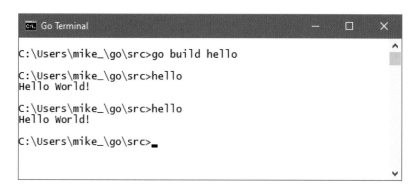

```
C:\Users\mike_\go\src>go build hello

C:\Users\mike_\go\src>hello
Hello World!

C:\Users\mike_\go\src>hello
Hello World!

C:\Users\mike_\go\src>_
```

Format and Comment Code

It is good practice to always ensure your Go source code is properly formatted by the **go fmt** tool before running a program.

It is also good practice to include explanatory comments in your source code so it can be more easily understood by others, and by yourself when revisiting the code later. Single-line comments can be added after a // character sequence – everything on the line after // is ignored by the compiler. Multi-line comments can be added between /* and */ character sequences – this is useful to "comment-out" blocks of code, to hide it from the compiler during development.

1. Edit the code in **hello.go** on page 14 to add a comment, and unnecessary tab spacing (bad formatting)

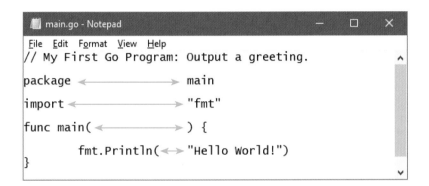

```
main.go - Notepad
File  Edit  Format  View  Help
// My First Go Program: Output a greeting.

package            main

import             "fmt"

func main(         ) {

        fmt.Println(  "Hello World!")
}
```

Beware

Comments should not be "nested", one inside another.

2. Now, at a prompt, enter the command **go fmt hello** then reopen the source code file to see correct formatting

```
Go Terminal
C:\Users\mike_\go\src>go fmt hello
hello\main.go
```

```
main.go - Notepad
File  Edit  Format  View  Help
// My First Go Program: Output a greeting.

package main

import "fmt"

func main() {

        fmt.Println("Hello World!")
}
```

Hot tip

The **go fmt** tool provides some simple error checking. For example, omit a final " double quote and it will provide the line number and position where the error occurs and provide the nature of the error as "string literal not terminated".

Explore the VS Code Editor

Although you can create Go programs just fine with a command prompt and plain text editor, many developers prefer to use a specialized code editor app. These offer useful additional features such as syntax highlighting, auto-indentation, bracket-matching and code debugging. Perhaps the best free code editor is the Visual Studio Code ("VS Code") app from Microsoft. It's available for download at **https://code.visualstudio.com/download** in versions for Windows, Linux and macOS.

When you download and install VS Code, you have only got the code editor framework. VS Code can actually support many different programming and scripting languages, so you have to install an appropriate extension for the one you want to code with.

1 Download and install VS Code

2 To open the "Extensions Marketplace" sidebar, first click **View, Appearance, Show Activity Bar**, then click the **Extensions** button on the Activity Bar

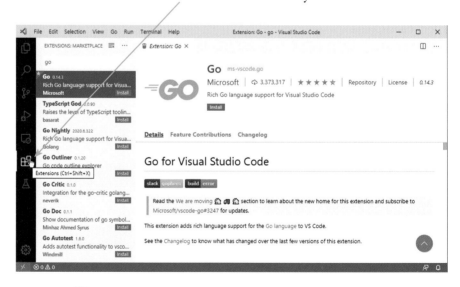

3 Next, type "go" into the search box to find the VS Code extension for the Go programming language

4 Click **Install** to add the Go language support to VS Code – if asked to add further Go support, select **Install All**

...cont'd

5 Click **File**, **Add Folder to Workspace** and add your "go" workspace folder containing the "src" folder with your source code

6 Click the **Explorer** button on the Activity Bar, then select a file to open in the main VS Code editor window – for example, click the **main.go** file in the "hello" folder

Hot tip

7 Click **View**, **Debug Console** to open an output panel – typically, this will appear below the code editor window, but can be moved

The VS Code app is highly customizable – you change the layout of its components to your liking and choose from several light or dark color themes. The screenshots shown here depict the default Light theme, and the syntax highlighting shown here in the code editor window is the same as that used throughout this book.

8 Click **Run**, **Run Without Debugging** to see the output appear in the Debug Console

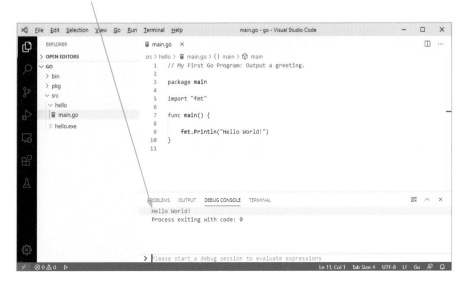

Summary

- Go programs are plain text files that get compiled into machine code to produce an executable binary version.

- The Go tools allow you to build, run, and test programs written in the Go programming language.

- The Go installation includes standard packages of useful, trusted code that you can import into programs.

- The command-line **go** command displays a list of the Go tool commands.

- The **GOROOT** environment variable stores the location on your system where the Go installation is located.

- The **GOPATH** environment variable stores the location on your system where your Go workspace is located.

- The Go workspace is a directory name "go", containing sub-directories named "src", "bin", and "pkg".

- The name of a Go package is that of the directory containing the Go source code files.

- A Go **package** declaration specifies its type, and must be specified as **package main** to be compiled into an executable.

- An **import** declaration quotes the name of any packages whose features are to be made available to the program.

- A function declaration contains the **func** keyword followed by the function name, **( )** parentheses, and **{ }** curly brackets.

- All Go programs must have a function named "main" as the entry point into the program.

- The **go run** command compiles and runs a program.

- The **go build** command compiles a program and produces an executable binary file that can be distributed.

- The **go fmt** command should be used to correctly format the source code of a Go package.

- VS Code offers features such as syntax highlighting, auto-indentation, bracket-matching, and code debugging.

2 Store Values

This chapter demonstrates how to store, retrieve, and manipulate various types of data using variable containers in Go programs.

Create Program Variables

A variable is a container in a Go program in which a data value can be stored inside the computer's memory. The stored value can be referenced using the variable's name and changed by assigning a new value. The programmer can choose any name for a variable providing it adheres to the naming convention rules listed below:

Naming Rule	Example
CANNOT be a Go keyword	**default**
CANNOT contain arithmetic operators	**a+b*c**
CANNOT contain punctuation characters	**%$#@!**
CANNOT contain any spaces	**no spaces**
MUST start with a letter	**msg**
CAN contain numbers elsewhere	**good1**
CAN contain mixed case	**camelCase**

Go keywords are listed in the table on the inner front cover of this book.

Variable names are case-sensitive in Go – so variables named "NUM", "Num", and "num" would be treated as three separate variables.

Variable names should be concise and should always begin with a lowercase letter – unless the variable is to be made accessible to other packages (more on this later). It is good practice to choose meaningful names for variables to make the program code more easily understood. To create a variable in the program simply requires it to be "declared" using the **var** keyword. A variable declaration has this syntax:

var *variableName dataType*

The **var** keyword is followed by a space then the chosen variable name, then the type of data this variable will be allowed to store. Typically, this will be one of the five data types described on the opposite page. Multiple variables of the same data type can be created in a single declaration as a comma-separated list, like this:

var *variableName1, variableName2, variableName3 dataType*

The basic data types in the Go language are defined using Go keywords. These types are listed in the table below, together with a description of each data type:

Data Type	Description	Example
string	A string of characters	"Hi there!"
int	An integer whole number	100
float64	A floating-point number correct to about 15 places	0.0123456789
byte	A single byte capable of storing just one character	'A'
bool	A boolean value of true or false	true

Character values of the **byte** data type must be enclosed by single quotes ' ' – double quotes are incorrect.

It is important to recognize that Go is a "statically typed" language, which means that a variable can only ever contain data of the type specified in its declaration.

When a value is assigned to a variable, that variable is said to have been "initialized". A variable can be declared then initialized later, or a variable may be initialized when it is declared. For example, to initialize a variable to contain a value of the **string** data type:

```
var msg string
msg = "Hi there!"

var msg string = "Hi there!"
```

Additionally, a variable can be declared and initialized using a special := operator. In this case, neither the **var** keyword nor data type is required, like this:

```
msg := "Hi there!"
```

The Go compiler simply infers the data type from the type of data being assigned to the variable. This is the preferred way to create and initialize a variable – but it can only be used inside the body of a function.

Short variable names are recommended in Go programming, so the examples here use **msg** rather than **message** for the variable name.

Display Variable Values

The value of variables can be displayed using the **fmt.Println( )** function that was used in Chapter 1 to display the "Hello World!" message. Alternatively, the desired format in which to display the variable value can be specified to a **fmt.Printf( )** function using a suitable "format specifier" and the variable name:

Specifier	Description	Example
%s	A string of characters	"Go Fun!"
%d	An integer -32768 to +32767	100
%f	A floating-point number	0.123456
%c	A single character	'A'
%t	A boolean value	true
%p	A machine memory address	0x0022FF34
%v	The value in a default format	*(any of the above)*
%T	The data type of the variable	int

The **%v** format specifier can be used to display any value, and the **%T** format specifier is useful to confirm the data type of any variable.

A format specifier can ensure that the output occupies a minimum number of spaces by stating the required number of spaces after the **%** character – for example, to ensure that an integer always fills at least seven spaces with the specifier **%7d**. If it is preferable for the blank spaces to be filled with zeros, just add a zero to make the specifier into **%07d**.

A precision specifier is a . full stop (period) followed by a number that can be used with the **%f** format specifier to determine how many decimal places to display – for example, to display two decimal places with **%.2f**. The precision specifier can be combined with the minimum space specifier to control the number of spaces and number of decimal places – for example, to display seven spaces including two decimal places and empty spaces filled by zeros with **%07.2f**. By default, empty spaces precede the number so it is right-aligned. They can also be added after the number to make it left-aligned by prefixing the minimum space specifier with a minus sign.

...cont'd

1 Create a directory named "vars" inside your "src" folder

2 Begin a **main.go** program with package and import declarations
package main
import "fmt"

src\vars\main.go

3 Add a main function that declares and initializes two variables
```
func main( ) {
    num := 100
    pi := 3.1415926536
    // Statements to be inserted here.
}
```

4 In the main function, insert statements to output the variable values in various formats
```
fmt.Printf( "num: %v type:%T \n", num, num )
fmt.Printf( "pi: %v type:%T \n\n", pi, pi )

fmt.Printf( "%%7d displays %7d \n", num )
fmt.Printf( "%%07d displays %07d \n\n", num )

fmt.Printf( "Pi is approximately %1.10f \n", pi )
fmt.Printf( "Right-aligned %20.3f rounded pi \n", pi )
fmt.Printf( "Left-aligned %-20.3f rounded pi \n", pi )
```

Hot tip

The **fmt.Printf( )** function does not add a new line after the output. You must manually include a \n newline escape sequence to move the printer head to the next line. To display a % character with the **fmt.Printf( )** function, prefix it with another **%** character as seen here.

5 Save the program file in the "vars" directory, then run the program to see the variable values in the specified formats

```
Go Terminal                                      —  □  ×

C:\Users\mike_\go\src>go run vars
num: 100 type:int
num: 3.1415926536 type:float64

%7d displays      100
%07d displays 0000100

Pi is approximately 3.1415926536
Right-aligned                3.142 rounded pi
Left-aligned 3.142               rounded pi

C:\Users\mike_\go\src>_
```

Beware

Notice that the floating-point value is rounded when the format specifier allocates fewer decimal places – it is not simply truncated.

25

Convert Data Types

You will sometimes need to convert the value stored in a variable to a different data type. Typically, you will want to convert a string value to a numerical value to perform an arithmetical operation. For example, a **string** might contain the numerical characters "42", but you cannot perform arithmetic on that value unless you convert it to an **int** or **float64** data type.

The Go standard library includes a **strconv** package containing functions that convert to and from the **string** data type. You make these functions available to your program by adding the **strconv** package to the import declaration.

The **strconv.Atoi( )** function converts a **string** specified within its parentheses into an **int** data type. It returns the **int** equivalent of the **string**, but like other functions you will meet in Go it also returns a second value that will be the special **nil** zero value when the conversion succeeds, or an error message if it fails. This means you must assign the call to the **strconv.Atoi( )** function to two variables to receive the two returned values, like this:

```
num, err := strconv.Atoi( "42" )
```

There is also a **strconv.Itoa( )** function that converts an **int** value to a **string** value, but this only returns the single **string** value.

If you prefer to convert a **string** value to a **float64** you can use the **strconv.ParseFloat( )** function. Like **strconv.Atoi( )** this returns the **float64** equivalent of a **string** and a **nil** value or error message. It requires the **string** value and the float size (**64**) as its arguments within its parentheses – for example, **strconv.ParseFloat("42", 64)**.

Casting conversion between different numeric data types is simply a matter of stating the required type followed by parentheses containing the value to be converted. For example:

```
var num int = 42
var decimal float64 = float64( num )
```

Interestingly, when a variable of the **byte** data type (an alias for **uint8** – an 8-bit unsigned integer) is assigned a single character it will store a numerical value that is the ASCII character code for that character, which can be easily cast to a **string** data type:

```
var char byte = 'A'
var str = string( char )
```

Hot tip

ASCII (pronounced as "as-kee") is an acronym for "American Standard Code for Information Interchange" and is the accepted standard for plain text. You can find the full range of standard ASCII codes at www.asciitable.com

1 Create a directory named "cast" inside your "src" folder

2 Begin a **main.go** program with package and import declarations

```
package main
import (
  "fmt"
  "strconv"
)
```

src\cast\main.go

3 Add a main function that declares and initializes two variables

```
func main( ) {
  var str string = "42"
   var char byte = 'A'
  // Statements to be inserted here.
}
```

You will discover later how to confirm that the conversion succeeded by testing that the **err** value is indeed **nil** – this is considered to be good practice throughout Go programming.

4 In the main function, insert statements to output the variable values after various conversions

```
num, err := strconv.Atoi( str )
fmt.Printf( "num:%v %T %v \n", num, num, err )

decimal := float64( num )
fmt.Printf( "decimal: %.2f %T \n", decimal, decimal )

fmt.Printf( "char:%v %T %v \n", char, char, string( char ) )
```

5 Save the program file in the "cast" directory, then run the program to see the variable values after conversion

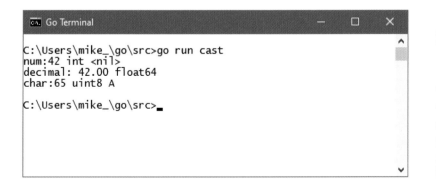

```
Go Terminal                                    —   □   ✕

C:\Users\mike_\go\src>go run cast
num:42 int <nil>
decimal: 42.00 float64
char:65 uint8 A

C:\Users\mike_\go\src>_
```

Values cast from a **float** to an **int** get truncated, so with **f := 3.9** and **n := int(f)** the variable **n** will be assigned **3** as its value.

1000000

Fix Constant Values

If you want to store a fixed value that will never change during the execution of your program, you should declare it using the **const** keyword, rather than the **var** keyword. This prevents accidental (or mischievous) attempts to assign a different value. The compiler will display a "cannot assign to" message if your code tries to assign a new value to a constant.

Unlike variable declarations, a constant declaration must be initialized with its fixed value in the declaration, like this:

const oneMillion = 1000000

Optionally, a constant declaration may specify a data type, but if an explicit data type is omitted from the declaration, the Go compiler will infer its type from the assigned value.

Multiple constants of the same, or different, data type can be created in a single declaration as a comma-separated list, like this:

const oneMillion, oneThousand = 1000000, "1,000"

Usefully, a constant declaration can employ a "constant generator" named **iota** to create a sequence of related constant values. The constant names should be listed one-per-line within parentheses after the **const** keyword, and the first one assigned the **iota** value. This generates a numerical sequence, beginning at zero, that increments by one for each named constant in the list. For example, you could assign a numeric sequence to constants representing days of the week, like this:

```
const (
  sunday = iota
  monday
  tuesday
  wednesday
  thursday
  friday
  saturday
)
```

Hot tip

In other programming languages, the generated sequence is often called an "enumeration" or simply "enum".

In this example, the constant **sunday** would be assigned zero (**0**), **monday** would be assigned one (**1**), and so on.

If you want to begin the sequence at a different number, simply add that number to **iota** in the assignment to the first constant.

1 Create a directory named "const" inside your "src" folder

2 Begin a **main.go** program with package and import declarations
```
package main
import "fmt"
```

src\const\main.go

3 Add a main function that declares and initializes a single constant and a sequence of constants, starting at one (**1**)
```
func main( ) {
    const pi = 3.14159

    const (
        red = iota + 1
        yellow
        green
        brown
        blue
        pink
        black
    )
    // Statements to be inserted here.
}
```

Hot tip

The **math** package in Go provides a constant named **math.Pi** that is a far better approximation of the value of π.

29

4 Next, insert statements to display several constant values
```
fmt.Printf( "Pi approximately: %v \n\n", pi)

fmt.Printf( "Red: %v point \n", red )
fmt.Printf( "Blue: %v points \n", blue )
fmt.Printf( "Black: %v points \n", black )
```

5 Save the program file in the "const" directory, then run the program to see the constant values

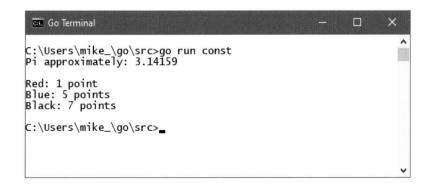

```
Go Terminal                                    —  □  ×

C:\Users\mike_\go\src>go run const
Pi approximately: 3.14159

Red: 1 point
Blue: 5 points
Black: 7 points

C:\Users\mike_\go\src>
```

Hot tip

The sequence here represents the points value of each ball in the game of snooker.

Point to Stored Values

Whenever your program creates a container to store data, your computer allocates a space in memory at which to store the data. Like houses, memory locations may be of different size but each one has a unique address.

An initialized variable therefore actually consists of three parts – name, value, and the memory address where the data is stored.

Go programming supports the concept of "pointers". A pointer variable can store the address of another variable and can access the value stored at that address.

The declaration of a pointer variable requires the data type to be prefixed by an * asterisk, to indicate that this will be a pointer:

var ptr *int   **// Declares this variable will point to an int.**

The address of another variable can be assigned to the pointer by prefixing the other variable's name with an **&** ampersand:

ptr = &num   **// Assigns an address to the pointer variable.**

The value at the assigned address can then be accessed by prefixing the pointer name with an * asterisk:

*ptr   **// Points to the value at the assigned address.**

The concept of pointers can be difficult to grasp because the * asterisk operator performs two purposes – as a type descriptor in a declaration, and as a dereferencer when placed before a pointer name. You may at this moment be thinking "Pointers, so what?" but pointers are widely used in Go programming, so you should thoroughly understand how they work before proceeding further.

Hot tip

Memory location addresses are hexadecimal numbers that are allocated by your computer. They will almost certainly differ on your system from the addresses shown in this example.

...cont'd

1   Create a directory named "point" inside your "src" folder

src\point\main.go

2   Begin a **main.go** program with package and import declarations
```
package main
import "fmt"
```

3   Add a main function that declares and initializes a regular integer variable and a pointer variable
```
func main( ) {
    var num int = 20
    var ptr *int = &num
    // Statements to be inserted here.
}
```

4   Next, insert statements to display the value and memory address of the regular integer variable
```
fmt.Printf( "num value: %v type: %T \n", num, num )
fmt.Printf( "num address: %v type: %T \n\n", ptr, ptr )
```

5   Now, insert statements to display the dereferenced value and memory address of the pointer variable
```
fmt.Printf( "num via pointer: %v type: %T \n", *ptr, *ptr )
fmt.Printf( "ptr address: %v type: %T \n\n", &ptr, &ptr )
```

Hot tip

The most important feature to recognize here is that the pointer changes the original value stored in the variable to which it points, not a copy of that value. This becomes significant when passing variables to functions – see pages 64-67.

6   Finally, insert statements to change the value stored in the integer variable – by assignment to the pointer variable
```
*ptr = 100
fmt.Printf( "new num value: %v type: %T \n", num, num )
```

7   Save the program file in the "point" directory, then run the program to see the variable values and addresses

```
Go Terminal                               —    □    ×

C:\Users\mike_\go\src>go run point
num value: 20 type: int
num address: 0xc00009e068 type: *int

num via pointer: 20 type: int
ptr address: 0xc0000c8018 type: **int

new num value: 100 type: int

C:\Users\mike_\go\src>_
```

Summary

- A variable stores data that can be referenced via the variable's given name, and its value can be changed.

- An explicit variable declaration uses the **var** keyword and states the type of data that variable can contain.

- An implicit variable declaration can be made inside a function body using the := operator to infer the data type.

- Go is a statically typed language in which a variable can only ever contain data of the type specified in its declaration.

- The **fmt.Printf( )** function can use format specifiers, variable names and **\n** newline escape sequences to format output.

- The **strconv.Atoi( )** function returns the **int** data type equivalent of a **string** value specified within its parentheses, and a second value that will be **nil** or an error message.

- The **strconv.Itoa( )** function returns the **string** data type equivalent of an **int** value specified within its parentheses.

- The **strconv.ParseFloat( )** function returns the **float64** data type equivalent of a **string** value specified within its parentheses, and a second value that will be **nil** or an error message.

- When a variable of the **byte** data type is assigned a character, it stores the ASCII character code number of that character.

- Casting between numeric data types states the required type followed by parentheses containing the value to be converted.

- A constant declaration uses the **const** keyword, and must be initialized with the fixed value it will contain.

- A pointer variable can store the memory address of another variable, and can access the value stored at that address.

- The * asterisk operator prefixes the data type in a pointer variable declaration to indicate that variable will be a pointer.

- The **&** ampersand operator prefixes the name of a regular variable to reference that variable's memory address.

- The * asterisk operator prefixes the name of a pointer variable to reference the value stored at the address it points to.

3 Perform Operations

This chapter introduces Go operators and demonstrates the operations they can perform.

Do Arithmetic

The arithmetic operators commonly used in Go programs are listed in the table below, together with the operation they perform:

Operator	Operation
+	Addition
-	Subtraction
*	Multiplication
/	Division
%	Remainder
++	Increment
--	Decrement

Don't forget

The **+** operator is dual-purpose – it is also used to concatenate strings.

The operators for assignment, addition, subtraction, multiplication, and division act as you would expect, but care must be taken to group expressions where more than one operator is used – operations within innermost **( )** parentheses are performed first:

```
a = b * c - d % e / f ;          // This is unclear.

a = ( b * c ) - ( ( d % e ) / f ) ;   // This is clearer.
```

The **%** remainder operator divides the first given number by the second given number and returns the remainder of the operation. This is useful to determine if a number has an odd or even value.

Hot tip

Values used with operators to form expressions are called "operands" – in the expression **2 + 3** the numerical values **2** and **3** are the operands.

The **++** increment operator and **--** decrement operator alter the given number by one and return the resulting value. These are most commonly used to count iterations in a loop – counting up on each iteration with the **++** increment operator, or counting down on each iteration with the **--** decrement operator.

The **++** increment or **--** decrement operator must be placed immediately after a variable name to alter its value. For example:

```
n := 4
n++               // Now n = 5.
```

1 Create a directory named "arith" inside your "src" folder

2 Begin a **main.go** program with package and import declarations

```
package main
import "fmt"
```

src\arith\main.go

3 Add a main function that declares and initializes two variables

```
func main( ) {
    a := 8
    b := 4
    // Statements to be inserted here.
}
```

4 In the main function, insert statements to output the sum resulting value after each arithmetical operation

```
fmt.Println( "Addition:\t", ( a + b ) )
fmt.Println( "Subtraction:\t", ( a - b ) )
fmt.Println( "Multiplication:\t", ( a * b ) )
fmt.Println( "Division:\t", ( a / b ) )
fmt.Println( "Remainder:\t", ( a % b ) )
```

Here, the \t escape sequence is used to output a tab space to align the results.

5 Now, insert statements to change the stored values and display their new value

```
a++
fmt.Println( "Increment:\t", a )
b--
fmt.Println( "Decrement\t", b )
```

6 Save the program file in the "arith" directory, then run the program to see the results of each operation

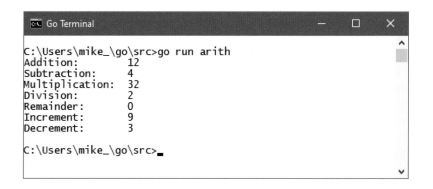

Assign Values

The operators that are used in Go programming to assign values are listed in the table below. All except the simple = assignment operator are a shorthand form of a longer expression, so each equivalent is given for clarity:

Operator	Example	Equivalent
=	a = b	a = b
+=	a += b	a = (a + b)
-=	a -= b	a = (a - b)
*=	a *= b	a = (a * b)
/=	a /= b	a = (a / b)
%=	a %= b	a = (a % b)

Don't forget

The += combined operator is dual-purpose – it can also be used to concatenate strings.

Beware

It is important to regard the = operator to mean "assign" rather than "equals" to avoid confusion with the == equality operator that is described on page 38.

In the assignment example above, where **a = b**, the variable named "a" is assigned the value that is contained in the variable named "b" – so that is then the value stored in the **a** variable. Technically speaking, the assignment operator stores the value of the right-hand operand in the memory location denoted by the left-hand operand, then returns the value as a result.

The **+=** combined operator is useful to add a value onto an existing value that is stored in a variable. In the example above, where **a += b**, the value in variable **b** is added to that in variable **a** – so the total is then the value stored in the **a** variable. The arithmetic operation is performed first with the grouped operands. The result is then stored in the memory location denoted by the first variable and returned.

All the other combined operators work in the same way by performing the arithmetical operation between the two values first, then assigning the result of that operation to the first variable – to become its new stored value.

With the **%=** combined operator, the grouped left-hand operand **a** is divided by the grouped right-hand operand **b**, then the remainder of that operation is assigned to the **a** first variable.

...cont'd

1 Create a directory named "assign" inside your "src" folder

2 Begin a **main.go** program with package and import declarations
```
package main
import "fmt"
```

src\assign\main.go

3 Add a main function that declares two variables
```
func main( ) {
    var a, b int
    // Statements to be inserted here.
}
```

4 In the main function, insert statements to output simply assigned values
```
a, b = 8, 4
fmt.Println( "Assigned Values:\ta =", a, "\tb =", b )
```

Notice here how multiple variables are initialized in a single statement.

Hot tip

5 Now, insert statements to change the value stored in the first variable and display its new value
```
a += b          // a = 8 + 4.
fmt.Println( "Add and Assign:\ta =", a )
a -= b          // a = 12 - 4.
fmt.Println( "Subtract and Assign:\ta =", a )
a *= b          // a = 8 * 4.
fmt.Println( "Multiply and Assign:\ta =", a )
a /= b          // a = 32 / 4.
fmt.Println( "Divide and Assign:\ta =", a )
a %= b          // a = 8 % 4.
fmt.Println( "Remainder Assigned:\ta =", a )
```

6 Save the program file in the "assign" directory, then run the program to see the results of each operation

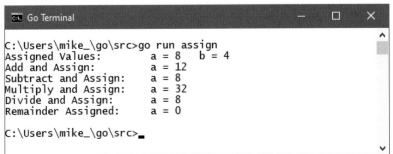

```
C:\Users\mike_\go\src>go run assign
Assigned Values:        a = 8    b = 4
Add and Assign:         a = 12
Subtract and Assign:    a = 8
Multiply and Assign:    a = 32
Divide and Assign:      a = 8
Remainder Assigned:     a = 0

C:\Users\mike_\go\src>
```

Beware

The operands must be of the same data type.

Make Comparisons

The operators that are commonly used in Go programming to compare two numerical values are listed in the table below:

Operator	Comparative Test
==	Equality
!=	Inequality
>	Greater than
<	Less than
>=	Greater than or equal to
<=	Less than or equal to

The comparison operators are also known as "relational operators".

The == equality operator compares two operands and will return **true** if both are equal in value, otherwise the == operator will return **false**. If both are the same number they are equal, or if both are characters their ASCII code values are compared numerically.

Conversely, the != inequality operator returns **true** if two operands are not equal, using the same rules as the == equality operator, otherwise it returns **false**. Equality and inequality operators are useful in testing the state of two variables to perform conditional branching in a program.

The > "greater than" operator compares two operands and will return **true** if the first is greater in value than the second, or it will return **false** if it is equal or less in value. The < "less than" operator makes the same comparison but returns **true** if the first operand is less in value than the second, otherwise it returns **false**. Typically, a > "greater than" or < "less than" operator is used to test the value of an iteration counter in a loop structure.

Adding the = assignment operator after a > "greater than" operator or a < "less than" operator makes them also return **true** if the two operands are exactly equal in value.

...cont'd

1 Create a directory named "comp" inside your "src" folder

src\comp\main.go

2 Begin a **main.go** program with package and import declarations

```
package main
import "fmt"
```

3 Add a main function that declares and initializes five variables

```
func main( ) {
    var zero, num, max int = 0, 0, 1
    var up, dn byte = 'A', 'a'
    // Statements to be inserted here.
}
```

The ASCII code value for uppercase **'A'** is 65 but for lowercase **'a'** it's 97 – so their comparison here returns **false**.

4 In the main function, insert statements to output the result of several comparisons

```
result := ( num == zero )        // 0 == 0.
fmt.Println( "Equality:\tnum == zero\t", result )

result = ( up == dn )            // A == a.
fmt.Println( "Equality:\tup == dn\t", result )

result = ( max != zero )         // 1 != 0.
fmt.Println( "Inequality:\tmax != zero\t", result )

result = ( zero > max )          // 0 > 1.
fmt.Println( "Greater:\tzero > max\t", result )

result = ( max <= zero )         // 1 <= 0.
fmt.Println( "Less or Equal:\tmax <= zero\t", result )
```

When comparing numbers, remember to test for equality as well as testing for higher and lower values.

5 Save the program file in the "comp" directory, then run the program to see the results of each comparison

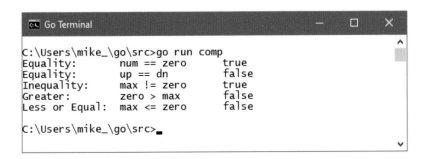

```
C:\Users\mike_\go\src>go run comp
Equality:       num == zero     true
Equality:       up == dn        false
Inequality:     max != zero     true
Greater:        zero > max      false
Less or Equal:  max <= zero     false

C:\Users\mike_\go\src>
```

Assess Logic

The logical operators most commonly used in Go programming are listed in the table below:

Operator	Operation
&&	Logical-AND
||	Logical-OR
!	Logical-NOT

The logical operators are used with operands that have boolean values of **true** or **false**, or are values that convert to **true** or **false**.

The **&&** logical-AND operator will evaluate two operands and return **true** only if both operands themselves are **true**. Otherwise, the **&&** logical-AND operator will return **false**. This is used in conditional branching where the direction of a program is determined by testing two conditions – if both conditions are satisfied, the program will go in a certain direction, otherwise it will take a different direction.

Unlike the **&&** logical-AND operator, which needs both operands to be **true**, the **||** logical-OR operator will evaluate its two operands and return **true** if either one of the operands itself returns **true**. If, however, neither operand returns **true**, then the **||** logical-OR operator will return **false**. This is useful in Go programming to perform a certain action if either one of two test conditions has been met.

The **!** logical-NOT operator is a unary operator that is used before a single operand. It returns the inverse value of the given operand, so if the variable **a** had a value of **true** then **!a** would have a value of **false**. The **!** logical-NOT operator is useful in Go programs to toggle the value of a variable in successive loop iterations with a statement like **a = !a**. This ensures that on each pass the value is changed, like flicking a light switch on and off.

The term "boolean" refers to a system of logical thought developed by the English mathematician George Boole (1815-1864).

① Create a directory named "logic" inside your "src" folder

src\logic\main.go

② Begin a **main.go** program with package and import declarations
package main
import "fmt"

③ Add a main function that declares and initializes two variables
func main( ) {
    var yes, no bool = true, false
    // Statements to be inserted here.
}

④ In the main function, insert statements to determine whether both variables contain **true** values
result := (yes && no)
fmt.Println("AND Logic:\tyes && no\t", result)

⑤ Next, insert statements to determine whether either of the variables contains a **true** value
result = (yes || no)
fmt.Println("OR Logic:\tyes || no\t", result)

⑥ Now, insert statements to display the current value of a variable and its inverse value
result = !yes
fmt.Println("NOT Logic:\tyes =", yes, "\t!yes =", result)

⑦ Save the program file in the "logic" directory, then run the program to see the results of logical assessments

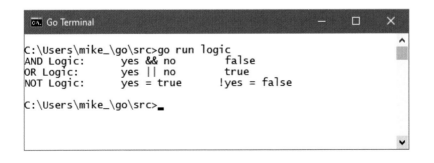

```
C:\Users\mike_\go\src>go run logic
AND Logic:      yes && no       false
OR Logic:       yes || no       true
NOT Logic:      yes = true      !yes = false

C:\Users\mike_\go\src>
```

Don't forget

The value returned by the ! logical-NOT operator is the inverse of the stored value – the stored value itself remains unchanged.

41

Hot tip

Comparing **false && false** returns **false**, not **true** – demonstrating the maxim "two wrongs don't make a right".

Juggle Bits

In computer terms, each byte comprises eight bits that can each contain a **1** or a **0** to store a binary number, representing decimal values from 0 to 255. Each bit contributes a decimal component only when that bit contains a **1**. Components are designated right-to-left from the "Least Significant Bit" (LSB) to the "Most Significant Bit" (MSB). The binary number in the bit pattern below is **00110010** and represents the decimal number 50 (2+16+32):

Bit No.	8 MSB	7	6	5	4	3	2	1 LSB
Decimal	128	64	32	16	8	4	2	1
Binary	0	0	1	1	0	0	1	0

It is possible to manipulate individual bit parts of a byte using the Go "bitwise" operators listed below:

Operator	Name	Example Operation
&	AND	0011 & 0101 = 0001
|	OR	0011 | 0101 = 0111
^	XOR	0011 ^ 0101 = 0110
^	NOT	^0101 = 1010
&^	AND NOT	0011 &^ 0101 = 0010
<<	Shift left	0010 << 2 = 1000
>>	Shift right	1000 >> 2 = 0010

By far the most common use of bitwise operators is to manipulate a compact "bit field" representing a set of boolean "flags". This is a much more efficient use of memory than storing boolean flag values in separate variables – a **byte** data type of just one byte can hold a bit field of eight flags, one per bit, whereas eight separate **byte** variables would require eight whole bytes of memory.

Don't forget

Many Go programmers never use bitwise operators but it is useful to understand what they are and how they may be used.

Hot tip

Each half of a byte is known as a "nibble" (4 bits). The binary numbers in the examples in the table describe values stored in a nibble.

...cont'd

1 Create a directory named "bits" inside your "src" folder

2 Begin a **main.go** program with package and import declarations
```
package main
import "fmt"
```

src\bits\main.go

3 Add a main function that declares and initializes one variable comprising eight bits
```
func main( ) {
    var flags byte = 10    // Binary 1010 (1x8 0x4 1x2 0x1).
    // Statements to be inserted here.
}
```

Larger bit fields with more bit flags can be created using a variable with more memory – an **int** data type is 32 bits wide on a 32-bit system and 64 bits wide on a 64-bit system.

4 In the main function, insert statements to output all the bit flag settings
```
fmt.Printf( "Flag #1:%v \n", ( flags & 1 ) > 0 )
fmt.Printf( "Flag #2:%v \n", ( flags & 2 ) > 0 )
fmt.Printf( "Flag #3:%v \n", ( flags & 4 ) > 0 )
fmt.Printf( "Flag #4:%v \n", ( flags & 8 ) > 0 )
```

5 Next, insert a statement to display the decimal value representing this pattern
```
fmt.Printf( "Flags Value: %08b \t%v \n", flags, flags )
```

6 Now, insert statements to shift the "on" bit flags one bit to the right and output the decimal value of the new pattern
```
flags = flags >> 1
fmt.Printf( "New Value: %08b \t%v \n", flags, flags )
```

The **%b** format specifier is used here to output the binary numerical value in each bit.

7 Save the program file in the "bits" directory, then run the program to see the bit flag values

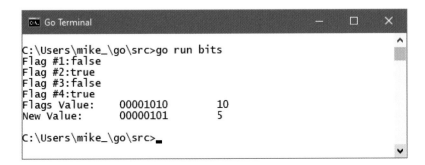

Understand Precedence

Operator precedence defines the order in which the Go compiler evaluates expressions. In the expression **6 + 7 * 3** the order of precedence determines whether the addition or the multiplication is completed first.

The table below lists operator precedence in decreasing order, where operators on higher rows have precedence over those on lower rows, so their operations get completed first. Binary operators on the same row have equal precedence but the order of completion is determined by their left-to-right order, so that operations on the left get completed first.

Precedence Level	Operator
5	* / % << >> &
4	+ - | ^
3	== != < <= >=
2	&&
1	||

The **++** increment operator and **--** decrement operator form statements in Go programming, rather than appear in expressions, so they are not included in the precedence table above.

You can force the compiler to ignore the default precedence levels by enclosing parts of an expression within parentheses, to force the compiler to evaluate innermost parts of the expression first. For example, in the expression **6 + 7 * 3** the * multiplication operator has, by default, a higher level of precedence than the + addition operator, so the multiplication operation is performed first as **7 * 3 = 21** then the addition **21 + 6 = 27**. You may prefer to have the addition operation performed first, so you can force the compiler to do that by adding parentheses to the expression as **(6 + 7) * 3**. Now, the evaluation of the expression is **6 + 7 = 13**, then the multiplication **13 * 3 = 39**.

...cont'd

① Create a directory named "force" inside your "src" folder

② Begin a **main.go** program with package and import declarations
package main
import "fmt"

src\force\main.go

③ Add a main function that declares and initializes a variable by evaluating an expression and displays its value
```
func main( ) {
    sum := 2 * 3 + 4 - 5
    fmt.Printf( "Default Order: %v \n", sum )
    // Statements to be inserted here.
}
```

④ In the main function, insert statements to display the value of evaluating a modified expression
```
sum = 2 * ( ( 3 + 4 ) - 5 )
fmt.Printf( "Forced Order: %v \n\n", sum )
```

⑤ Next, insert a statement to display the value of evaluating another expression
```
sum = 7 % 3 * 2
fmt.Printf( "Default Order: %v \n", sum )
```

⑥ Now, insert statements to display the value of evaluating another modified expression
```
sum = 7 % ( 3 * 2 )
fmt.Printf( "Forced Order: %v \n\n", sum )
```

⑦ Save the program file in the "force" directory, then run the program to see the different outcomes

Hot tip

Use parentheses in your expressions to avoid unexpected results.

```
Go Terminal                          —   □   ×

C:\Users\mike_\go\src>go run force
Default Order: 5
Forced Order: 4

Default Order: 2
Forced Order: 1


C:\Users\mike_\go\src>
```

Summary

- Arithmetical operators can form expressions with two operands for addition +, subtraction -, multiplication *, division /, and remainder %.

- Increment ++ and decrement -- operators modify a single operand by a value of one.

- The assignment = operator can be combined with an arithmetical operator to perform an arithmetical calculation then assign its result.

- Comparison operators can form expressions comparing two operands for equality ==, inequality !=, greater >, < lesser, greater or equal >=, and lesser or equal <= values.

- Logical-AND && and logical-OR || operators form expressions evaluating two operands to return a boolean value of **true** or **false**.

- The logical-NOT ! operator returns the inverse boolean value of a single operand.

- A single memory byte comprises eight bits, which may each contain a value of one (1) or zero (0).

- Bitwise operators OR |, AND &, NOT ~, and XOR ^ each return a value after comparison of the values within two bits.

- The shift left << and shift right >> operators move the bit values a specified number of bits in their direction.

- The most common use of bitwise operators is to manipulate a compact bit field containing a set of boolean flags.

- Expressions containing multiple operators will perform their operations in accordance with the default precedence level unless explicitly forced by the addition of parentheses.

4 Control Flow

Test a Condition

The **if** keyword is used to perform the basic conditional test that evaluates a given expression for a boolean value of **true** or **false**. Statements within **{ }** curly brackets following the evaluation will only be executed when the expression's condition is found to be **true**. The syntax of an **if** test statement looks like this:

if *test-expression* {
        statements-to-execute-when-the-condition-is-true
}

There may be multiple statements to be executed when the test is **true** but each statement must be on its own line. Sometimes it may be desirable to evaluate multiple expressions to determine whether following statements should be executed. This can be achieved using the logical **&&** AND operator with this syntax:

if *test-expression* **&&** *test-expression* {
        statements-to-execute-when-all-conditions-are-true
}

Alternatively, multiple **if** statements can be "nested", one inside another, to evaluate multiple expressions, like this:

if *test-expression* {
  if *test-expression* {
        statements-to-execute-when-all-conditions-are-true
  }
}

When one or more expressions evaluated by an **if** test statement are found to be **false**, the statements in its following curly brackets are not executed and the program proceeds to subsequent code. It is often preferable to extend an **if** statement by appending an **else** statement specifying statements within curly brackets to be executed when the expressions evaluated by the **if** statement are found to be **false**, with this syntax:

if *test-expression* {
        statements-to-execute-when-the-condition-is-true
} else {
        statements-to-execute-when-the-condition-is-false
}

This is a fundamental programming technique that offers the program two directions in which to proceed, depending on the result of the evaluation, and is known as "conditional branching".

Beware

The test expression and opening **{** curly bracket must appear on the same line as the **if** keyword.

Beware

The **else** keyword and opening **{** curly bracket must appear on the same line as the **}** closing curly bracket of the previous block of statements.

1 Begin a main function with a statement that tests whether two characters are matching

```go
func main( ) {

    if 'A' == 'A' {
        fmt.Println( "\nCharacters Match" )
    }

    // Statements to be inserted here.

}
```

src\ifelse\main.go

2 Next, in the main function, insert nested statements to test two numerical expressions

```go
if 5 > 1 {
    if 7 > 2 {
        fmt.Println( "\nBoth expressions are true" )
    }
}
```

To avoid repetition, the code listed in the steps from this point on now assumes you have declared **package main** and **import "fmt"** at the start of each program.

3 Now, insert statements to test a numerical expression and to test whether two characters are not matching

```go
if 5 < 1 {
    fmt.Println( "\n1st Condition is true" )
} else if 'A' != 'A' {
    fmt.Println( "\n2nd Condition is true" )
} else {
    fmt.Println( "\nBoth Conditions are false" )
}
```

Notice that you can use **else if** to evaluate a second expression if the first test is **false**.

4 Save the program file in an "ifelse" directory, then run the program to see the results of the conditional tests

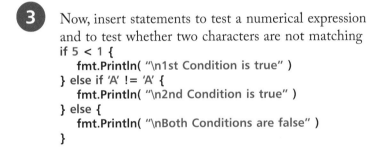

```
Go Terminal                                    —  □  ×

C:\Users\mike_\go\src>go run ifelse

Characters Match

Both Expressions are true

Both Conditions are false

C:\Users\mike_\go\src>_
```

Switch Cases

Conditional branching performed by multiple **if else** statements can often be performed more efficiently by a **switch** statement when the test expression just evaluates a single condition.

The **switch** statement works in an unusual way. It takes a given value as its parameter argument then seeks to match that value from a number of **case** statements. Code to be executed when a match is found is included in each **case** statement.

It is important that each statement to be executed must appear on its own line, starting on the line below the **case** statement.

Optionally, the list of **case** statements can be followed by a single final **default** statement to specify code to be executed in the event that no matches are found within any of the **case** statements. So the syntax of a switch statement typically looks like this:

```
switch test-value {
  case match-value :
         statements-to-execute-when-matched
  case match-value :
         statements-to-execute-when-matched
  case match-value :
         statements-to-execute-when-matched
  default :
         statements-to-execute-when-no-match-found
}
```

Where a number of match-values are to each execute the same statements, only the final **case** statement need include the statements to be executed. For example, to output the same message for match-values of 0, 1, and 2:

```
switch num {
  case 0 :
  case 1 :
  case 2 :
         fmt.Println( "Less than 3" )
  case 3 :
         fmt.Println( "Exactly 3" )
  default :
         fmt.Println( "Greater Than 3 or Less Than 0" )
}
```

A **default** statement need not appear at the end of the **switch** block but it is logical to place it there.

When a match is found, the **switch** normally ends, but you can add the **fallthrough** keyword as a final statement in any **case** block to continue to the next **case** statement – although this is seldom useful.

1 Begin a main function with a statement that declares and initializes two variables

```go
func main( ) {
    num := 2
    char := 'B'

    // Statements to be inserted here.
}
```

src\switch\main.go

2 Next, in the main function, insert a statement that tries to match a numerical value

```go
switch num {
    case 1 :
        fmt.Println( "\nNumber is One" )
    case 2 :
        fmt.Println( "\nNumber is Two" )
    case 3 :
        fmt.Println( "\nNumber is Three" )
    default :
        fmt.Println( "\nNumber is Unrecognized" )
}
```

3 Now, insert a statement that tries to match a character

```go
switch char {
    case 'A' :
        fmt.Println( "\nLetter is A" )
    case 'B' :
        fmt.Println( "\nLetter is B" )
    default :
        fmt.Printf( "\nLetter is Unrecognized" )
}
```

Hot tip

You can also omit the test value after the **switch** keyword in a "tagless switch". This is the equivalent of **switch true** – to seek a case that evaluates as **true**.

4 Save the program file in a "switch" directory, then run the program to see the results of the conditional tests

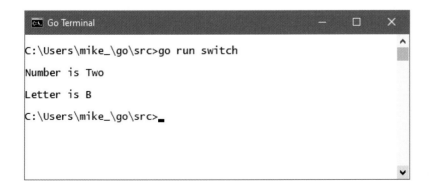

```
Go Terminal                                    —    □    ×

C:\Users\mike_\go\src>go run switch

Number is Two

Letter is B

C:\Users\mike_\go\src>
```

51

Loop Several Times

A loop is a piece of code in a program that automatically repeats. One complete execution of all statements within a loop is called an "iteration", or a "pass". The length of a loop is controlled by a conditional test made within the loop. While the tested expression is found to be **true**, the loop will continue – until the tested expression is found to be **false**, at which point the loop ends.

In Go programming, there are several ways to construct a loop but they all use the **for** keyword. The most common type of loop statement begins with three components – an initializer, a single test expression, and an incrementer, with this syntax:

for *initializer* ; *test-expression* ; *incrementer* **{**
      statements-to-be-executed

}

The initializer is used to set a starting value for a counter of the number of iterations to be made by the loop. An integer variable is used for this purpose and is traditionally named "i".

Upon each iteration of the loop, the test-expression is evaluated, and that iteration will only continue while this expression is **true**. When the test-expression becomes **false**, the loop ends immediately without executing the statements again. With every iteration the counter is incremented then the statements executed.

Loops can be nested, one within another, to allow complete execution of all iterations of an inner nested loop on each iteration of the outer loop. A second integer variable is used to count the iterations of the inner loop, and is traditionally named "j". Should that inner loop also contain a nested loop, its counter is traditionally named "k", and the syntax looks like this:

for *initializer* ; *test-expression* ; *incrementer* **{**
      statements-to-be-executed

      for *initializer* ; *test-expression* ; *incrementer* **{**
            statements-to-be-executed

            for *initializer* ; *test-expression* ; *incrementer* **{**
                  statements-to-be-executed
            }
      }
}

Nesting loops beyond three levels is uncommon and is probably best avoided.

1 Begin a main function with a loop that performs five iterations

```go
func main( ) {

    for counter := 1 ; counter <= 5 ; counter++ {
        fmt.Println( "Loop Iteration", counter )
    }

    // Statements to be inserted here.
}
```

src\forloop\main.go

2 Next, insert a loop that performs three iterations

```go
for i := 1 ; i <= 3 ; i++ {
    fmt.Println( "\nOuter Loop Iteration", i )
    // Inner Loop to be inserted here.
}
```

3 Now, insert an inner loop that performs three iterations

```go
for j := 1 ; j <= 3 ; j++ {
    fmt.Println( "\tInner Loop Iteration", j )
}
```

4 Save the program file in a "forloop" directory, then run the program to see the output on each loop iteration

```
Go Terminal                                  —  □  ✕

C:\Users\mike_\go\src>go run forloop
Loop Iteration 1
Loop Iteration 2
Loop Iteration 3
Loop Iteration 4
Loop Iteration 5

Outer Loop Iteration 1
        Inner Loop Iteration 1
        Inner Loop Iteration 2
        Inner Loop Iteration 3

Outer Loop Iteration 2
        Inner Loop Iteration 1
        Inner Loop Iteration 2
        Inner Loop Iteration 3

Outer Loop Iteration 3
        Inner Loop Iteration 1
        Inner Loop Iteration 2
        Inner Loop Iteration 3

C:\Users\mike_\go\src>_
```

Hot tip

A **for** loop counter can also count down – by decrementing the counter value on each iteration using **i--** instead of **i++**.

Loop While True

An alternative to the **for** loop described in the previous example on page 53 only contains a test expression after the **for** keyword – it does not include an initializer or incrementer at the beginning of the loop statement. Instead, it uses a counter variable that has already been initialized, and increments the counter within the body of the loop. This is the Go equivalent of a "while" loop in other programming languages, as the loop will continue iterating while the test expression remains **true**. The incrementer must at some point render the test expression **false** to end the loop, or an infinite loop will have been created that will never end. The syntax of this type of **for** loop looks like this:

initializer
for *test-expression* {
      statements-to-be-executed
      incrementer
}

A further variation of a loop structure in Go programming allows you to even omit the test expression from the beginning statement and use an infinite loop with a test expression contained in the loop body. It too uses a counter variable that has already been initialized, and increments the counter within the body of the loop. This is the Go equivalent of a "do-while" loop in other programming languages, as the loop will execute its statements and continue iterating while the test expression remains **true**. When the test expression becomes **false**, the loop can be terminated using the **break** keyword, so the syntax of this type of **for** loop looks like this:

initializer
for {
      statements-to-be-executed
      incrementer
      if *test-expression* {
            statements-to-be-executed
            break
      }
}

Notice that a "while" loop will not make a single iteration if the test expression is **false** on its first evaluation, whereas a "do-while" loop will always make at least one iteration because its statements are executed before the evaluation is made.

Hot tip

In the event that a program runs an infinite loop, on Windows or Linux systems press the **Ctrl** + **C** keyboard keys to halt the loop execution.

...cont'd

1 Begin a main function with a loop that performs five iterations

```go
func main( ) {

    counter := 1
    for counter <= 5 {
        fmt.Println( "Loop Iteration", counter )
        counter++
    }
    // Statements to be inserted here.
}
```

src\while\main.go

2 Next, insert an infinite loop statement

```go
i := 10
for {
    fmt.Println( "\t\t\tCountdown", i )
    i--
    // Test expression to be inserted here.
}
```

Change the initial value of the **i** variable to **0** (zero) and run the program again to see the first iteration of the loop get executed.

3 Now, insert a test expression to end the loop

```go
if i < 1 {
    fmt.Println( "\t\t\t\tLift Off!" )
    break
}
```

4 Save the program file in a "while" directory, then run the program to see the output on each loop iteration

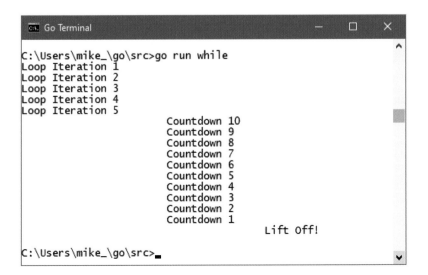

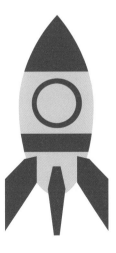

55

Break Out of Loops

The **break** keyword can be used to prematurely terminate any loop when a specified condition is met. The **break** statement is situated inside the loop statement block and is preceded by a test expression. When the test returns **true**, the loop ends immediately and the program proceeds on to the next task. For example, in a nested inner loop it proceeds to the next iteration of the outer loop.

The **continue** keyword can be used to skip a single iteration of a loop when a specified condition is met. The **continue** statement is situated inside the loop statement block and is preceded by a test expression. When the test returns **true**, that single iteration ends.

src\break\main.go

1. Begin a main function with a loop that performs three iterations
```go
func main( ) {
    for i := 1 ; i <= 3 ; i++ {
        // Inner Loop to be inserted here.
    }
}
```

2. Insert an inner loop that performs three iterations
```go
// Statements to be inserted here.
for j := 1 ; j <= 3 ; j++ {
    fmt.Println( "Running i=", i, "j=", j )
}
```

3. Save the program file in a "break" directory, then run the program to see the output on each loop iteration

Hot tip

You can also **break** to a label at a specific point outside of nested code blocks – see an example of this on page 166.

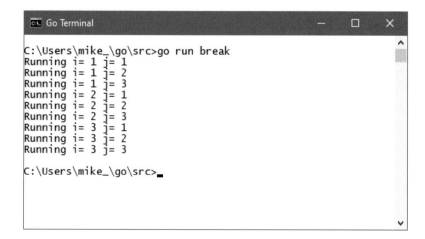

```
Go Terminal                                        —    □    X

C:\Users\mike_\go\src>go run break
Running i= 1 j= 1
Running i= 1 j= 2
Running i= 1 j= 3
Running i= 2 j= 1
Running i= 2 j= 2
Running i= 2 j= 3
Running i= 3 j= 1
Running i= 3 j= 2
Running i= 3 j= 3

C:\Users\mike_\go\src>
```

4 Next, insert this **break** statement at the very beginning of the inner loop block, to break out of the inner loop

```
if i == 2 && j == 2 {
    fmt.Println( "Breaks When i=", i, "and j=", j )
    break
}
```

5 Save the updated file, then run the program again to see the inner loop terminate on its second iteration

```
Go Terminal                                    —    □    ×

C:\Users\mike_\go\src>go run break
Running i= 1 j= 1
Running i= 1 j= 2
Running i= 1 j= 3
Running i= 2 j= 1
*                    Breaks When i= 2 and j= 2
Running i= 3 j= 1
Running i= 3 j= 2
Running i= 3 j= 3

C:\Users\mike_\go\src>_
```

Don't forget

Here, the **break** statement halts the second and third iterations of the inner loop when the outer loop tries to run it for the second time.

6 Now, insert this **continue** statement before the **break** statement – to skip the second iteration of the inner loop

```
if i == 3 && j == 2 {
    fmt.Println( "Continues When i=", i, "and j=", j )
    continue
}
```

7 Save the updated file, then run the program once more to see only the second iteration of the inner loop skipped

```
Go Terminal                                    —    □    ×

C:\Users\mike_\go\src>go run break
Running i= 1 j= 1
Running i= 1 j= 2
Running i= 1 j= 3
Running i= 2 j= 1
*                    Breaks When i= 2 and j= 2
Running i= 3 j= 1
*                    Continues When i= 3 and j= 2
Running i= 3 j= 3

C:\Users\mike_\go\src>_
```

Don't forget

Here, the **continue** statement just skips the second iteration of the inner loop when the outer loop tries to run it for the third time.

Go to Labels

The **goto** keyword at first glance seems like a great feature, as it allows the program flow to jump to a label at any position in the program code, much like a hyperlink on a web page. However, in reality this can cause errors, its use is frowned upon, and it is generally considered bad programming practice.

The **goto** keyword jump is a powerful feature that has existed in computer programs for decades, but its power was abused by many early programmers who created programs that jumped around in an unfathomable manner. This produced unreadable program code, so the use of **goto** became hugely unpopular.

Typically, the program might execute a sequence of statements, then a **goto** statement would jump back to a label at the beginning of the sequence to repeat their execution. Additionally, a condition might be tested at some point during the sequence, and a further **goto** statement might jump to a point after the sequence to continue the program flow if the tested condition was not met. In this way, the program code quickly gained lots of confusing **goto** statements and labels.

One possible valid use of the **goto** keyword is to break cleanly from an inner nested loop by jumping to a label just after the end of its outer loop block. This immediately exits both loops so no further iterations of either loop are executed.

src\jump\main.go

1 Begin a main function with a loop that performs three iterations
```go
func main( ) {
    for i := 1 ; i <= 3 ; i++ {
        // Inner Loop to be inserted here.
    }
}
```

2 Insert an inner loop that performs three iterations
```go
for j := 1 ; j <= 3 ; j++ {
    fmt.Println( "Running i=", i, "j=", j )
}
```

3 Save the program file in a "jump" directory, then run the program to see the output on each loop iteration

```
Go Terminal                                    —    □    ×

C:\Users\mike_\go\src>go run jump
Running i= 1 j= 1
Running i= 1 j= 2
Running i= 1 j= 3
Running i= 2 j= 1
Running i= 2 j= 2
Running i= 2 j= 3
Running i= 3 j= 1
Running i= 3 j= 2
Running i= 3 j= 3

C:\Users\mike_\go\src>
```

Beware

Avoid creating a program executable named "goto.exe" as this may conflict with the internal **GOTO** command on Windows systems.

4 Insert a statement as the first line of the inner nested loop, to jump to a label named "end" at a specified counter value

```
if i == 2 && j == 2 {
    goto end
}
```

5 Now, add the label on the next line after the closing **}** brace of the outer loop

end:

Don't forget

Notice that the label itself must end with a : colon character.

6 Save the updated file, then run the program once more to see the loop end when the tested condition becomes **true**

```
Go Terminal                                    —    □    ×

C:\Users\mike_\go\src>go run jump
Running i= 1 j= 1
Running i= 1 j= 2
Running i= 1 j= 3
Running i= 2 j= 1

C:\Users\mike_\go\src>
```

Summary

- The **if** keyword performs a basic conditional test to evaluate a given expression for a boolean value of **true** or **false**.

- The **else** keyword can be used to provide alternative statements to execute when an **if** statement finds an expression to be **false**.

- Offering a program alternative directions in which to proceed following an evaluation is known as "conditional branching".

- Conditional branching performed by multiple **if else** statements can often be performed more efficiently by a **switch** statement.

- The statements within a **switch** block must each appear on a separate line below the **case** statement.

- Optionally, a **switch** block may contain a **default** statement specifying statements to execute when no match is found.

- The **for** keyword can specify an initializer, a test-expression, and an incrementer, to control a loop.

- The **for** keyword can simply specify a test expression to determine whether a loop should continue while **true**.

- The **for** keyword can entirely omit the test-expression to create an infinite loop.

- A condition can be tested within the body of an infinite loop to end the loop with the **break** keyword.

- The **break** keyword can be used to terminate a loop, whereas the **continue** keyword can be used to skip a single iteration.

- Loops may be nested so that inner loops perform a sequence of iterations upon each iteration of their outer loop.

- Use of the **goto** keyword is generally not recommended, but it can legitimately be used to exit from nested loops.

5 Produce Functions

Create a Basic Function

Previous examples in this book have used the obligatory **main( )** function and functions contained in the Go standard library, such as the **fmt.Println( )** function in the "fmt" package. However, most Go programs contain a number of custom functions, which can be called as required during the execution of the program.

A function block simply contains a group of statements that get executed whenever that function is called. Once the function statements have been executed, program flow resumes at the point directly following the function call. This modularity is very useful in Go programming to isolate set sequences of code that can be called upon repeatedly as required.

To add a custom function into a Go program it must be declared using the **func** keyword, followed by a name of your choice – adhering to the same naming conventions used for variable names.

Naming Rule	Example
CANNOT be a Go keyword	**default**
CANNOT contain arithmetic operators	**a+b*c**
CANNOT contain punctuation characters	**%$#@!**
CANNOT contain any spaces	**no spaces**
MUST start with a letter	**msg**
CAN contain numbers elsewhere	**good1**
CAN contain mixed case	**camelCase**

Beware

Function names should begin with a lowercase letter unless the function is to be exported – see page 78.

When choosing a function name it should describe the purpose of the function but be concise. The function name is followed by ( ) parentheses and an { opening curly bracket, all on the same line. This line is often referred to as the function "signature". The statements to be executed are contained in the function body, and the body ends with a } closing curly bracket – just as with the **main** function. The function can be called within a program by stating its name followed by ( ) parentheses.

...cont'd

1 Create a function that will simply print a message each time it gets called

```go
func first( ) {

    msg := "Hello from the 1st function!"
    fmt.Println( msg )
}
```

src\funcs\main.go

2 Create another function that will simply print the result of a multiplication each time it gets called

```go
func sqFive( ) {

    fmt.Printf( "%v \n", 5 * 5 )
}
```

The listed code assumes you have declared **package main** and **import "fmt"** at the start of each program.

3 Next, add a **main** function that begins with a statement that calls the **first** function to print its message

```go
func main( ) {

    first( )

    // Statements to be inserted here.
}
```

4 Now, insert statements to display a multiplication sum and print its result

```go
fmt.Print( "5 x 5 = " )
sqFive( )
```

5 Save the program file in a "funcs" directory, then run the program to see the printed output

```
Go Terminal                              —  □  ✕

C:\Users\mike_\go\src>go run funcs
Hello from the 1st function!
5 x 5 = 25

C:\Users\mike_\go\src>_
```

Variables declared inside a function or other block are only accessible from within that block – they have "local scope". For example, here the **msg** variable is only accessible from within the **first( )** function. Variables declared outside a function block are accessible from anywhere in the program – they have "global scope". It is preferable to use only local variables to avoid possible conflicts with variables existing in global scope.

63

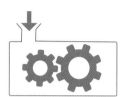

Add Parameters

The ( ) parentheses that follow the function name in a function declaration can, optionally, contain a comma-separated list of "parameters". These are variables that can be used by the function but whose initial content is supplied by the caller. The variables are created whenever the function gets called, and are destroyed when control exits from the function. Each parameter must be given a name of your choice, following the usual variable naming conventions, and a type with this syntax:

func *functionName* (*paramName type, paramName type*) {

      statements-to-be-executed

}

Multiple consecutive parameters of the same type can be declared as a list and need only specify the type after the final parameter of the same type, like this:

func *functionName* (*paramName, paramName type*) {

      statements-to-be-executed

}

Each function call must specify content for each parameter, of the correct type and in the same order as they appear in the function declaration. The contents being passed to the function are known as "arguments". These are specified as a comma-separated list within the ( ) parentheses following the function name in the call:

functionName (*argument, argument, argument*)

Unlike some other programming languages, Go has no way to specify default content for function parameters.

It is very important to recognize that in Go programming, arguments are, by default, passed "by value" – the function receives a copy of the argument, not the original argument. This means that changes made to the parameter variables do not, by default, affect the original argument specified by the caller – they only affect the copy.

1 Create a function that requires a single integer argument and displays its value

```go
func square( num int ) {

    fmt.Println( "\t\tReceived Copy:", num )

    // Statements to be inserted here.
}
```

src\args\main.go

2 Next, insert statements to modify the received argument and display its new value

```go
num = num * num
fmt.Println( "\t\tModified Copy:", num )
```

3 Begin a main function that declares and initializes a single variable, then displays its value

```go
func main( ) {
    num := 5
    fmt.Println( "Original:", num )

    // Statements to be inserted here.
}
```

You can also create "variadic functions" that accept any number of arguments – see page 106 for an example.

4 Now, insert statements in the main function to call the other function and once more display its variable value

```go
square( num )
fmt.Println( "Original:", num )
```

5 Save the program file in an "args" directory, then run the program to see the original value is unchanged

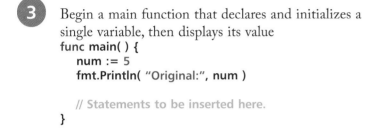

```
Go Terminal                              —    □    ×

C:\Users\mike_\go\src>go run args
Original: 5
                Received Copy: 5
                Modified Copy: 25
Original: 5

C:\Users\mike_\go\src>_
```

Pass References

The example on page 65 demonstrates that in Go programming arguments are, by default, passed "by value" – the function receives a copy of the argument, not the original argument. But quite often you may wish a function to modify the original argument. This can be achieved by passing an argument to the function that is a reference to the original, rather than a copy of its value.

Remember that pointers are a reference to the memory address on your system where a value has been stored. This means that if you pass a pointer argument to a function, it will be able to modify the original value residing at the address provided by the pointer.

When declaring a function that can receive pointer arguments, a data type specified in its parameter list must be prefixed by an * asterisk, to indicate that this parameter will be a pointer, like this:

func *functionName* (*paramName *type*) **{**

       statements-to-be-executed
}

The parameter will then be able to store a location address.

The function statements can access and modify a value at the address provided by the pointer, by prefixing the parameter name with an * asterisk as a dereferencer.

When calling a function that accepts a pointer argument, the argument must be prefixed with an **&** ampersand character to reference the memory address at which the value is stored.

This technique can be used with the **int**, **float64**, **string**, and **bool** data types, and also with the **struct** type that will be introduced in the next chapter. These are all "value types", so pointers are required to access the original values they contain when passing them to functions.

This technique cannot be used with **pointer** or **function** types (yes, functions are types in Go) nor with the **slice**, **map**, or **channel** types that are demonstrated later in this book. These are all already "reference types", so pointers are not required to access the original values they contain when passing them to functions.

Hot tip

Refer back to pages 30-31 for a refresher on how pointers work.

1 Create a function that requires a single integer pointer argument and displays its value

```go
func square( num *int ) {

    fmt.Println( "\t\tReceived Address:", num )

    // Statements to be inserted here.

}
```

src\refs\main.go

2 Next, insert statements to modify the received argument and display its new value

```go
*num = *num * *num
fmt.Println( "\t\tModified Original:", *num )
```

3 Begin a main function that declares and initializes a single variable, then displays its value

```go
func main( ) {
    num := 5
    fmt.Println( "Original:", num )

    // Statements to be inserted here.

}
```

4 Now, insert statements in the main function to call the other function and once more display its variable value

```go
square( &num )
fmt.Println( "Original:", num )
```

Add the **&** ampersand prefix when passing a pointer argument in a function call if you need to pass in the memory address at which a value is stored.

5 Save the program file in a "refs" directory, then run the program to see the original value is changed

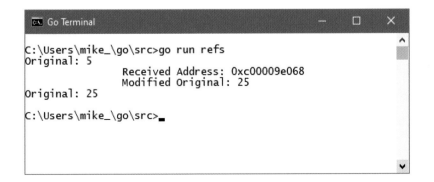

```
C:\Users\mike_\go\src>go run refs
Original: 5
                Received Address: 0xc00009e068
                Modified Original: 25
Original: 25

C:\Users\mike_\go\src>
```

Return Values

The functions described so far in this chapter simply resume the program flow at the next statement after the function call, but it is often useful to have a function return a value to the caller before continuing to execute subsequent statements.

When declaring a function that will return a value, the function signature must define the data type of the return value after its parameter list. The value to be returned is specified, typically at the end of a function body, to the Go **return** keyword. The syntax of a function that will return a single value looks like this:

func *funcName* (*paramName type*) *returnType* {

      statements-to-be-executed

      return *returnValue*

}

Unlike most other programming languages that can only return one value, functions in Go programming can return multiple values. When you want to return multiple values, the data type of each value must be specified as a comma-separated list in parentheses after the parameter list. The values to be returned are specified, typically at the end of a function body, to the Go **return** keyword. The syntax of a function that will return two values looks like this:

func *funcName* (*paramName type*) (*returnType, returnType*) {

      statements-to-be-executed

      return *returnValue, returnValue*

}

The values specified to the **return** keyword must each be of the same type specified in the function signature, and they must be listed in the same order.

If you call a function that returns multiple values but doesn't use all the returned values in your subsequent program code, the compiler will produce a "declared but not used" message, and the program will not run. To avoid this, you can assign any unwanted returned values to an _ underscore character. This is called a "blank identifier" in Go programming.

Many functions within the standard Go library return multiple values, especially to return both result and error values.

...cont'd

1 Create a function that requires a single integer argument and returns three values to the caller

```go
func cube( num int ) ( string, int, int ) {

    return "Result", num, ( num * num * num )
}
```

src\returns\main.go

2 Add a main function that assigns three returned values to three variables, then tries to display just two values

```go
func main( ) {
    a, b, c := cube( 5 )
    fmt.Println( b, "Cubed =", c )
}
```

3 Save the program file in a "returns" directory, then run the program to see a compiler error message

```
C:\Users\mike_\go\src>go run returns
# returns
returns\main.go:7:2: a declared but not used

C:\Users\mike_\go\src>
```

4 Modify the assignment in the main function to assign the first returned value to a blank identifier

```go
func main( ) {
    _, b, c := cube( 5 )
    fmt.Println( b, "Cubed =", c )
}
```

The returned "Result" **string** value is not used in the output here.

5 Save the program file once more, then run the program to see two returned values printed in the output

```
C:\Users\mike_\go\src>go run returns
5 Cubed = 125

C:\Users\mike_\go\src>
```

Call Recursively

Statements within custom functions can freely call other custom functions just as readily as they can call standard Go library functions like **fmt.Printf( )**. Additionally, functions can call themselves "recursively". As with loops, it is important that recursive function calls must modify a tested expression to avoid continuous execution – so the function will exit at some point.

Recursive function calls can be used to emulate loop structures, such as the countdown example on page 55:

src\recur\main.go

1 Create a function that requires an integer argument and makes recursive calls until that value is decremented to zero

```go
func countDn( num int ) {

    if num < 1 {
        fmt.Println( "\t\t\t\tLift Off!" )
    } else {
        fmt.Println( "\t\t\tCountdown", num )
        num--
        countDn( num )
    }
}
```

2 Add a main function that contains a statement to call the function above

```go
func main( ) {
    countDn( 10 )
}
```

3 Save the program file in a "recur" directory, then run the program to see recursive function calls emulate a loop

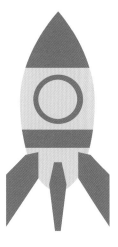

```
Go Terminal                                    —   □   ×
C:\Users\mike_\go\src>go run recur
                Countdown 10
                Countdown 9
                Countdown 8
                Countdown 7
                Countdown 6
                Countdown 5
                Countdown 4
                Countdown 3
                Countdown 2
                Countdown 1
                            Lift Off!

C:\Users\mike_\go\src>_
```

...cont'd

Recursive function calls are useful to resolve mathematical problems, such as the calculation of the factorial of a given number. The factorial is the multiplication of all integers from the given number down to one – e.g. the factorial of 3 is 6 (**3 * 2 * 1**).

1 Create a function that requires an integer argument and will return one integer value upon each call
```go
func facto( num int ) int {
    // Statements to be inserted here.
}
```

src\facto\main.go

2 Next, insert a statement to return a one (**1**) when the argument value is decremented to zero (**0**)
```go
if num == 0 {
    return 1
}
```

3 Then, insert a final statement to recursively call the function, to multiply all numbers in the sequence
```go
return num * facto( num - 1 )
```

4 Add a main function that contains a statement to print out seven factorials
```go
func main( ) {

    for i := 1 ; i <= 7 ; i++ {
        fmt.Println( "Factorial", i, "=", facto( i ) )
    }
}
```

Beware

Recursive functions are useful, but not very efficient. This example calls the **facto( )** function 35 times to generate this sequence of just 7 factorials!

5 Save the program file in a "facto" directory, then run the program to see a factorial sequence

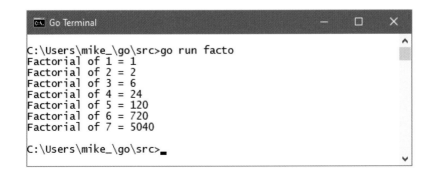

```
Go Terminal                            —   □   ×

C:\Users\mike_\go\src>go run facto
Factorial of 1 = 1
Factorial of 2 = 2
Factorial of 3 = 6
Factorial of 4 = 24
Factorial of 5 = 120
Factorial of 6 = 720
Factorial of 7 = 5040

C:\Users\mike_\go\src>_
```

Enclose Anonymously

The Go programming language has support for "first class functions". This allows functions to be assigned to variables, passed as arguments to other functions, and returned from functions.

Anonymous Functions

An anonymous function is simply a function definition that does not contain a name. This is useful to create a function inline without having to name it. Anonymous functions are also known as "function literals". Like other functions, these can contain a parameter list, return type list, and can return multiple values. You can create a self-invoking anonymous function expression by appending the ( ) call operator at the end of the function definition, like this:

```
func( ) { fmt.Println( "Function Literal" ) } ( )
```

Additionally, an anonymous function can be assigned to a variable, then called by appending the ( ) call operator after the variable name, like this:

```
fn := func( ) { fmt.Println( "Function Literal" ) }
fn( )
```

Closures

Perhaps the most useful purpose of anonymous functions is for the creation of "closures". A closure is a function nested inside an outer function that retains access to variables declared in the outer function. The outer function can return an anonymous function that retains access to the variables but, crucially, the variables are not accessible from anywhere else in the program code. This is a form of encapsulation that protects the data stored in those variables as the returned anonymous function "closes over" them.

The closure can be made self-invoking for assignment to a variable by appending the ( ) call operator after the end of the outer function definition. The anonymous inner function can then be called by appending the ( ) call operator after the variable name – and can access the persistent value in the outer function.

It can be difficult to grasp the concept of closures, as it would seem that the variable in the outer function should be destroyed when the self-invoking function has completed execution.

Hot tip

Self-invoking function expressions execute their statements one time only.

Hot tip

Don't worry if you can't immediately understand how closures work. They can seem mystical at first, but will become clearer with experience. You can continue on and come back to this technique later.

1 Begin a main function by assigning an anonymous function to a variable

```go
func main( ) {
    area := func( length, width int ) int {
        return length * width
    }
}
```

src\anon\main.go

2 Next, insert statements to display the anonymous function's type and two returned values

```go
fmt.Printf( "area Type: %T \n", area )
fmt.Println( "Area 1:", area( 10, 4 ) )
fmt.Println( "Area 2:", area( 12, 5 ) )
```

3 Now, insert statements to assign an anonymous self-invoking closure function to a variable

```go
counter := func( ) func( ) int {
    num := 0
    return func( ) int {
        num++
        return num
    }
} ( )
```

Notice that the outer function must state its return type as **func( ) int** because it will return a function that will in turn return an integer value.

73

4 Finally, insert statements to display the closure function's type and three returned values

```go
fmt.Printf( "counter type: %T \n", counter )
fmt.Println( "Count:", counter( ) )
fmt.Println( "Count:", counter( ) )
fmt.Println( "Count:", counter( ) )
```

5 Save the program file in an "anon" directory, then run the program to see the function types and returned values

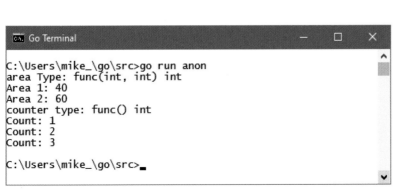

```
C:\Users\mike_\go\src>go run anon
area Type: func(int, int) int
Area 1: 40
Area 2: 60
counter type: func() int
Count: 1
Count: 2
Count: 3

C:\Users\mike_\go\src>
```

Pass Functions

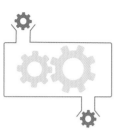

Programmer-defined Function Types

The output from the previous example on page 73 describes the function by its signature, for example, **counter type : func( ) int**. You can declare a custom function type using the **type** keyword, followed by a type name of your choice, and a function signature. For example, a custom function named "adder" that must receive two integer arguments and return one integer argument, like this:

type adder func(int, int) int

Variables can then be created as "instances" of the custom function type, and be assigned a function definition – whose signature must match that in the custom function type declaration. The function (instance) can be called in the usual way.

Higher-order Functions

Regular functions that receive value or reference arguments, and return these types to the caller, are called "first-order" functions. But functions can also be passed as arguments to other functions, and functions can return functions to the caller. Any function that accepts functions as arguments, or any function that returns one or more functions, is regarded as a "higher-order" function.

Passing functions to other functions allows actions to be modified without repeating existing lines of code.

src\ftype\main.go

1 Begin a main function by declaring a custom function type that has a signature requiring two integer arguments and an integer return type
```
func main( ) {

    type adder func( int, int ) int
}
```

2 Next, insert a statement to define a function (instance) of the custom function type – with a matching signature
```
var add adder = func( a int, b int ) int {
    return a + b
}
```

3 Now, insert a statement that calls the function (instance)
```
fmt.Println( "Added:", add( 6, 2 ) )
```
// Statements to be inserted here – Steps 6-8.

4 After the main function, begin a higher-order function that will both receive and return a function of the same signature as the custom function type

```go
func dub( twice func( int, int ) int ) func( int, int ) int {
    fmt.Println( "Doubled:", twice( 6, 2 ) * 2 )
    // Statements to be inserted here – Step 5.
}
```

5 Next, insert statements to define and return a function, of the same signature, to the caller

```go
div := func( a int, b int ) int {
    return ( a + b ) / 2
}
return div
```

Notice that a function signature need only state required types in the declaration, but its definition also needs to state parameter names.

6 Back in the main function, insert a statement to pass the function (instance) to the higher-order function, and assign that function's returned function to a variable

```go
div := dub( add )
```

7 Now, insert a statement that calls the returned function

```go
fmt.Println( "Divided:", div( 6, 2 ) )
```

8 Finally, insert statements to display the types of the function (instance), the higher-order function, and the returned function

```go
fmt.Printf( "add type: %T \n", add )
fmt.Printf( "dub type: %T \n", dub )
fmt.Printf( "div type: %T \n", div )
```

9 Save the program file in an "ftype" directory, then run the program to see the returned values and function types

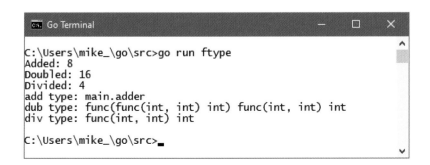

Notice that the function instance **add** is simply described as being of the custom function type **main.adder**.

Handle Errors

It is important to anticipate errors in your Go programs and enable your code to handle them efficiently. Other programming languages, such as Java and Ruby, throw "exceptions" when an error is encountered, which the program can try to catch at runtime, but Go provides a simpler approach.

Go programming allows you to handle errors that arise in functions by returning separate values. This makes it easy to identify which function is returning the error, and lets you handle the error using the familiar Go language constructs.

To handle a possible error, the function signature must include a Go built-in **error** return type. Traditionally, this is the final return value in the list of return values.

func *funcName* (*paramName type*) (*returnType*, **error**)

In place of the expected return value in the function body, the function can return a trivial value, such as **-1**, together with the returned error value.

If an error does not arise, the function can return the expected return value, together with a **nil** zero value. In Go programming, the **nil** zero value is used to represent a zero value for many types. Here, it simply indicates that that there was no error. The syntax of a function that handles errors might, therefore, look like this:

func *funcName* (*paramName type*) (*returnType*, **error**) {

```
    if condition != true {
            return -1 , errorValue
    }

    return returnValue, nil
}
```

Hot tip

The Go standard library also has an **errors** package that can be used to manipulate custom errors.

The "fmt" package that provides the **fmt.Println( )** and **fmt.Printf( )** functions, used in previous examples, also provides a **fmt.Errorf( )** function that returns an error type. This accepts the same format specifiers as the **fmt.Printf( )** function and can be used to return a message to identify the location and nature of an error.

1 Create a function that requires an integer argument and will return an integer value and an error

```go
func isPosInt( num int ) ( int, error ) {

    // Statements to be inserted here.

}
```

src\err\main.go

2 Next, insert a conditional test to return an error, or the argument value – depending on its value

```go
if num < 1 {
    err := fmt.Errorf( "%v not a positive integer", num )
    return -1, err
}
return num, nil
```

3 Now, add a main function that contains a decrementing loop to print out argument values or error messages

```go
func main( ) {

    for i := 2 ; i >= -2 ; i-- {
        res, err := isPosInt( i )

        if err != nil {
            fmt.Println( "Failed:", err )
        } else {
            fmt.Println( res, "Passed!" )
        }
    }
}
```

You will see the test **if err != nil** used in many Go programs as the standard way to begin an error handler.

4 Save the program file in an "err" directory, then run the program to see the error messages when the test fails

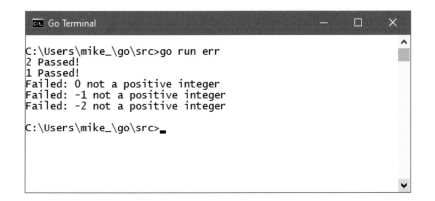

```
C:\Users\mike_\go\src>go run err
2 Passed!
1 Passed!
Failed: 0 not a positive integer
Failed: -1 not a positive integer
Failed: -2 not a positive integer

C:\Users\mike_\go\src>
```

Separate Files

As your programs increase in size it is often sensible to separate related sections of code into individual files. You can simply add a file in the same package directory as the **main.go** file and, providing it begins by declaring itself to belong to the same package (**package main**), any code in the added file will be treated as though it is contained in the **main.go** file.

When creating utility functions that may be useful to many programs, it is more appropriate to store these in a file contained in a separate package that can be imported into any program.

With imported custom packages it is important to recognize that only functions and variables whose name begins with a capital letter will be accessible from the importing file.

To use a function in an imported file, the function name must be prefixed by the package name, just as with the **fmt.Printf( )** function imported from the "fmt" package.

The example on page 77 could, for instance, be separated into two packages so the validation function could be exported.

1 First, begin a **verify.go** utility file with package and import declarations
```
package verify
import "fmt"
```

src\verify\verify.go

2 Add the validation function – but change its name to begin with a capital letter
```
// IsPosInt tests for positive argument.
func IsPosInt( num int ) ( int, error ) {
    if num < 1 {
        err := fmt.Errorf( "%v not a positive integer", num )
        return -1, err
    }
    return num, nil
}
```

Hot tip

Creating a Go archive package means that the utility file need not be recompiled each time an importing file is compiled.

3 Save the file in a "verify" directory inside your "src" folder

4 Enter the command **go install verify** to create a compiled archive file named "verify.a" within your **go/pkg** folder

5 Next, begin a **main.go** program with package and import declarations

```
package main
import (
  "fmt"
  "verify"
)
```

src\prog\main.go

6 Now, add the main function, prefixing the amended imported function name by its package name

```
func main( ) {

    for i := 2 ; i >= -2 ; i-- {
        res, err := verify.IsPosInt( i )

        if err != nil {
            fmt.Println( "Failed:", err )
        } else {
            fmt.Println( res, "Passed!" )
        }
    }
}
```

7 Save the program file in a "prog" directory, then enter the command **go build prog** to create a compiled executable file named "prog.exe" (on Windows) in your **go/src** folder

8 Finally, enter the command **prog** (**./prog** on Linux) to run the program and see the error messages when the test fails

When importing multiple packages, the import declaration must list them on individual lines between parentheses.

```
Go Terminal                          —   □   ✕

C:\Users\mike_\go\src>go install verify

C:\Users\mike_\go\src>go build prog

C:\Users\mike_\go\src>prog
2 Passed!
1 Passed!
Failed: 0 not a positive integer
Failed: -1 not a positive integer
Failed: -2 not a positive integer

C:\Users\mike_\go\src>_
```

Summary

- A function block contains a group of statements that get executed whenever that function is called.

- A function can be declared using the **func** keyword followed by a name that adheres to the Go naming conventions.

- A function declaration contains ( ) parentheses, followed by { } curly brackets to surround the statements to be executed.

- The parentheses in a function declaration may contain a parameters list that specifies the type of each parameter.

- Arguments passed to a function are, by default, passed by value – a copy of the original value.

- Pointer arguments passed to a function are a reference to a memory address that is the location of the original value.

- The **return** keyword allows one, or more, values to be returned to the caller after a function has executed its statements.

- If a function returns values to the caller, each return type must be listed after the parameter list in the function declaration.

- A function can call itself recursively to emulate a loop structure, but must test a condition to exit at some point.

- Go supports first class functions that can be assigned to variables, passed as arguments, and returned from functions.

- An anonymous function has no name and can be made self-invoking by appending the ( ) call operator after the block.

- A closure is a function nested inside an outer function that retains access to variables declared in the outer function.

- The **type** keyword followed by a name and function signature can be used to create a custom function type.

- Passing functions to other functions allows actions to be modified without repeating existing lines of code.

- Go programming allows you to handle errors that arise in functions by returning separate values.

- Only imported functions and variables whose names begin with a capital letter will be accessible to the importing file.

6 Build Structures

Group Data

Multiple related items of any data type can be grouped together in a Go language "struct" (structure) type. This is useful to create records, similar to those you might find in a database.

A struct is created using the **type** keyword, followed by a name of your choice, and the **struct** keyword followed by **{ }** curly brackets. The curly brackets contain a list of variable name and data type pairs on individual lines. These are known as the "fields" of the struct and define what the struct will contain, with this syntax:

type *structName* **struct** {

      fieldName dataType
      fieldName dataType

}

Hot tip

You can think of a struct as a template whose instances are copies that can hold actual data.

Having defined a **struct** type, instances of the struct can be created as variables declared with the name of the struct as their type:

var *instanceName structName*

Individual fields of a struct are addressed by appending the field name to the struct name using dot-suffixing. Data can be assigned to individual fields of the struct instance in several ways. Firstly, you can assign values to individual fields, like this:

instanceName.fieldName = value
instanceName.fieldName = value

Alternatively, you can initialize all its fields in a single statement that assigns a "struct literal" to an instance, like this:

instanceName = structName { value, value }

Using this technique requires the values to be listed in the same order as the fields in the struct, but you can include field names in the struct literal so the values may appear in any order, like this:

instanceName = structName { fieldName : value, fieldName : value }

Additionally, you can create a struct instance and initialize all its fields in a single statement that assigns a "struct literal" to a variable, like this:

instanceName := structName { fieldName : value, fieldName : value }

Empty fields in a struct get a zero value by default.

Beware

Although these two statements are similar, notice that the := operator is used only when creating an instance and initializing the struct fields in a single statement.

...cont'd

1 Start a program by creating a struct type
```
type employee struct {
    id int
    name string
    dept string
}
```

src\group\main.go

2 Next, begin the main function by creating an instance of the struct type
```
var coder employee
```

3 Now, assign values to each field of the struct instance
```
coder.id = 001
coder.name = "Alice"
coder.dept = "I.T."
```

4 Create a second instance of the struct, which initializes each field of the struct using a struct literal and field names
```
clerk := employee{ name: "Burt", dept: "Payroll", id: 002 }
```

5 Add statements to display all values in each struct group
```
fmt.Println( coder )
fmt.Println( clerk )
```

Note that the statement in Step 4 does not assign field values in the same order the fields are listed in the struct, but using field names ensures that values get assigned to the correct field.

6 Finally, add statements to display individual field values in a string
```
fmt.Printf( "\n%v works in %v \n", coder.name, coder.dept )
fmt.Printf( "\n%v works in %v \n", clerk.name, clerk.dept )
```

7 Save the program file in a "group" directory, then run the program to see the struct field values

```
Go Terminal                                    —    □    ✕

C:\Users\mike_\go\src>go run group
{1 Alice I.T.}
{2 Burt Payroll}

Alice works in I.T.

Burt works in Payroll

C:\Users\mike_\go\src>_
```

Attach Methods

In Go programming, functions can be attached to structs by adding a "receiver" to the function signature, which specifies a parameter name and the struct name as its type:

func (*paramName structName* **)** *funcName***( )**

A function that is attached to a struct is referred to as a "method" of that struct. The method can be specified as a value receiver, which operates on a copy of the struct, or as a pointer receiver that operates on the original struct fields:

func (paramName *structName) funcName( )

This ability enables structs to represent real-world objects that have attributes and behaviors:

● Attributes describe the features that an object has.

● Behaviors describe actions that an object can perform.

For example, a car might be described with attributes of "blue" and "coupe", along with an "accelerate" behavior.

These features could be represented in Go programming with a **car** struct containing field properties of **color** and **body**, along with an attached **accelerate( )** method.

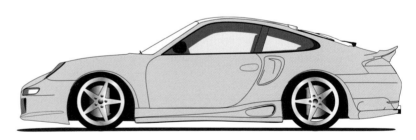

Objects are created in Go programming by defining a struct as a template from which different copies, or "instances", can be made.

Each instance of the struct can be customized by assigning attribute values and behaviors to describe that object.

Don't forget

Unlike some other programming languages, Go does not have classes, but can represent objects using structs instead.

...cont'd

1 Start a program by creating a struct type

```go
type car struct {
    color string
    body string
}
```

src\method\main.go

2 Next, attach a method to the struct type

```go
func ( c car ) accelerate( ) string {
    return "accelerating-->"
}
```

3 Now, begin the main function by creating two instances of the struct type

```go
porsche := car{ color: "blue", body: "coupe" }
bentley := car{ color: "green", body: "saloon" }
```

Hot tip

4 Add statements to display all values of the first instance

```go
fmt.Println( "Porsche paint is", porsche.color )
fmt.Println( "Porsche style is", porsche.body )
fmt.Println( "Porsche is", porsche.accelerate( ) )
```

When you call a method, Go automatically handles the conversion between values and pointers, so the receiver here could be (c *car) if you wanted the method to be able to modify the original struct fields.

5 Finally, add statements to display all values of the second instance

```go
fmt.Println( "Bentley paint is", bentley.color )
fmt.Println( "Bentley style is", bentley.body )
fmt.Println( "Bentley is", bentley.accelerate( ) )
```

6 Save the program file in a "method" directory, then run the program to see the struct field values

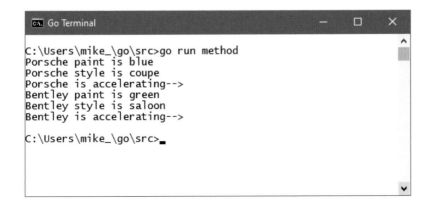

```
C:\Users\mike_\go\src>go run method
Porsche paint is blue
Porsche style is coupe
Porsche is accelerating-->
Bentley paint is green
Bentley style is saloon
Bentley is accelerating-->

C:\Users\mike_\go\src>
```

Embed Structs

As a struct field is declared simply with a name and type, and a struct is a type, Go programming even allows you to embed one struct within another by declaring a field to be of a struct type.

type *structName* **struct {**

       fieldName embeddedStructName

}

This is useful to build structures that efficiently use structs whose purpose can be varied. For example, take a struct that simply stores X and Y coordinates:

type coords struct {
      x, y int
}

This might be used to store a location on a chart, the corner point of a rectangle, etc., or perhaps the center point in a circle when embedded in another struct, like this:

type circle struct {
      radius int
      center coords
}

Now, when an instance of the circle is created, the fields of the embedded struct can be addressed by chaining together the struct names and field names, like this:

instanceName.embeddedStructName.fieldName
instanceName.embeddedStructName.fieldName

This is acceptable, but not very convenient as it's quite lengthy. Fortunately, Go provides a solution to this problem by supporting "anonymous fields" in structs. These are simply fields that specify the name of another struct as a field, without stating a field name:

type circle struct {
      radius int
      coords
}

The advantage of this is that it allows you to shorten the code required to address the fields of an embedded struct:

instanceName.fieldName
instanceName.fieldName

An anonymous field must be of a named type, or be a pointer to a named type.

1 Start a program by creating two struct types
```
type coords struct {
    x, y int
}

type circle struct {
    radius int
    coords
}
```

src\embed\main.go

2 Next, attach a method to the second struct
```
func ( c circle ) getDiameter( ) int {
    return c.radius * 2
}
```

3 Now, begin the main function by creating an instance of the struct type
```
var ring circle
```

4 Add statements to assign values to the struct field and embedded struct fields
```
ring.radius = 15
ring.x = ring.radius
ring.y = ring.radius
```

5 Finally, add statements to display values
```
fmt.Printf( "Diameter:%v \n", ring.getDiameter( ) )
fmt.Printf( "Point X:%v Y:%v \n", ring.x, ring.y )
```

6 Save the program file in an "embed" directory, then run the program to see the struct field values

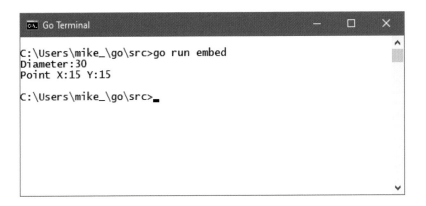

```
C:\Users\mike_\go\src>go run embed
Diameter:30
Point X:15 Y:15

C:\Users\mike_\go\src>
```

Encapsulate Features

The ability to represent objects in Go programs is the first cornerstone principle in Object Oriented Programming (OOP). An object-oriented program uses methods to express the properties and operations of the data structure to which it is attached, so the program need not access the object directly.

A variable, function, or method, that is not directly accessible to the program is said to be "encapsulated". Encapsulation, inheritance, and polymorphism are the three building-blocks of object-oriented programming.

Encapsulation in Go programming relies upon data-hiding in packages that are imported into a program. Only variable names, function names, and method names that begin with a capital letter will be exported to the program. Those that begin with a lowercase letter will be inaccessible – i.e. they are encapsulated.

src\cube\cube.go

1 First, begin a **cube.go** utility file with a package declaration and a struct definition

```
package cube

// Dims exportable.
type Dims struct {
    width, length, height int
}
```

2 Next, add four functions to operate on the struct fields

```
func ( d *Dims ) area( ) int {
    return d.width * d.length
}

// SetSize exportable.
func ( d *Dims ) SetSize( w, l, h int ) {
    d.width = w
    d.length = l
    d.height = h
}

// GetVolume exportable.
func ( d *Dims ) GetVolume( ) int {
    return d.width * d.length * d.height
}

// GetArea exportable.
func ( d *Dims ) GetArea( ) int {
    return d.area( )
}
```

Hot tip

See that fields of the same data type can be declared as a comma-separated list, as with variable declarations.

88

...cont'd

3 Save the utility file in a "cube" directory, then begin a main file that imports the utility file

```
package main

import (
    "cube"
    "fmt"
)
```

src\encap\main.go

4 Next, begin the main function by creating an instance of the imported struct type

```
var box cube.Dims
```

5 Now, call an imported method to assign values to the struct fields

```
box.SetSize( 2, 4, 6 )
```

Don't forget

You must prefix the imported struct with its package name. The instance could also be created by assigning an (empty) struct literal as **box := cube.Dims{ }.**

6 Then, call the other two imported methods to calculate results using the assigned field values

```
fmt.Println( "Footprint:", box.GetArea( ) )
fmt.Println( "Volume:", box.GetVolume( ) )
```

7 Save the program file in an "encap" directory, then run the program to see the results from encapsulated values

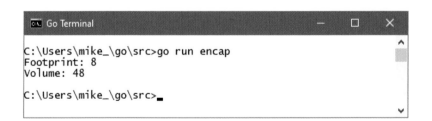

```
Go Terminal                                        —   □   ×

C:\Users\mike_\go\src>go run encap
Footprint: 8
Volume: 48

C:\Users\mike_\go\src>
```

8 Add these statements to the main function, which attempt to reference an unexported field and method

```
fmt.Println( "Width:", box.width )
fmt.Println( "Area:", box.getArea( ) )
```

9 Save the program file once more, then run the program to see compilation fail with **box.width undefined** and **box.getArea undefined** error messages

Compose Elements

The second cornerstone of object-oriented programming is that of inheritance, in which an object derived from another object will inherit the features of the base object. This code reuse is made possible in Go programming by "composition". This is simply the technique of embedding one struct inside another to instantly provide various elements to the second struct. For example, a "dog" struct might embed a base "animal" struct whose fields and attached methods become instantly available to the "dog" struct.

Strictly speaking, the fields and attached methods are not actually inherited from the base struct, but are made accessible to a second struct – i.e. they are, in a manner of speaking, "inherited".

src\inher\main.go

1 Start a program by creating a base struct with two fields
```
type member struct {
    firstName string
    lastName string
}
```

2 Next, attach a method to return the base struct field values, concatenated around a single space
```
func ( m member ) fullName( ) string {
    return m.firstName + " " +  m.lastName
}
```

3 Now, create a second struct with two further fields and the base struct embedded
```
type article struct {
    title string
    body string
    member
}
```

4 Then, attach a method to the second struct to output all field values
```
func ( a article ) content( ) {
    fmt.Println( "Title:", a.title )
    fmt.Println( "Content:", a.body )
    fmt.Printf( "Author: %v \n\n", a.fullName( ) )
}
```

5 Begin a main function by creating an instance of the base struct, initialized with a struct literal

```
func main( ) {

    member1 := member {
    "Mike",
    "McGrath",
    }
    // Statements to be inserted here.
}
```

6 Next, create an instance of the second struct and display all its field values

```
article1 := article {
    "Object Oriented Programming",
    "In Go, Composition emulates Inheritance",
    member1,
}
article1.content( )
```

Remember that all values in a struct literal must be followed by a comma – including the final one.

7 Now, create another instance of the second struct and display all its field values

```
article2 := article {
    "Object Oriented Programming",
    "Coming next... Polymorphism",
    member1,
}
article2.content( )
```

8 Save the program file in an "inher" directory, then run the program to see the values from inherited fields

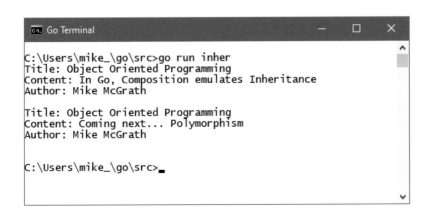

Satisfy Interfaces

The third cornerstone of object-oriented programming is that of "polymorphism" – a term derived from Greek, meaning "many forms", that describes the ability to assign a different meaning or purpose to an entity according to its context.

Go programming supports polymorphism with an "interface" type that is created using the **type** keyword, followed by a name of your choice and the **interface** keyword followed by **{ }** curly brackets. The interface body contains only a list of method signatures:

```
type interfaceName interface {
        methodName returnType
        methodName returnType
}
```

Any struct that has methods that precisely match the name and signature of all methods listed in the interface will implement that interface. In Go programming terms, they are said to "satisfy" the interface. The advantage of this is that it allows the program to have various structs with like-named attached methods that each perform a different task – i.e. they are polymorphic.

src\poly\main.go

1 Start a program by creating an interface that lists two method signatures, that each require no arguments and that each return a string

```
type bird interface {
    speak( ) string
    move( ) string
}
```

2 Next, create an empty struct and attach methods that will satisfy the interface

```
type parrot struct { }

func ( parrot ) speak( ) string {
    return "Squawk, squawk!"
}

func ( parrot ) move( ) string {
    return "A parrot flies away."
}
```

Hot tip

Notice that you can omit a parameter name from the receiver and simply state the struct name, unless you need to use a parameter name in a method statement.

...cont'd

3 Now, create another empty struct and attach methods that will also satisfy the interface

```go
type chicken struct { }

func ( chicken ) speak( ) string {
    return "Cluck, cluck!"
}

func ( chicken ) move( ) string {
    return "Chickens cannot fly."
}
```

Hot tip

Go automatically recognizes when an interface is implemented.

4 Add a function that receives the interface as an argument and calls the implemented methods

```go
func nudge( b bird ) {
    fmt.Printf( "\n%v \n", b.speak( ) )
    fmt.Printf( "%v \n\n". b.move( ) )
}
```

Don't forget

When a struct implements an interface, the methods attached to the struct become "honorary members" of the interface – so that when the interface is passed as an argument, the function can call those methods via its interface parameter.

5 Add a main function with statements that create instances of each struct, then call their like-named methods

```go
func main( ) {
    var bird1 parrot
    var bird2 chicken
    nudge( bird1 )
    nudge( bird2 )
}
```

6 Save the program file in a "poly" directory, then run the program to see the different outputs

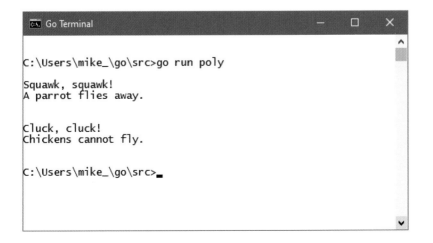

```
Go Terminal                          —  □  ×

C:\Users\mike_\go\src>go run poly

Squawk, squawk!
A parrot flies away.

Cluck, cluck!
Chickens cannot fly.

C:\Users\mike_\go\src>_
```

Embed Interfaces

Just as structs can be embedded in other structs, so can interfaces be embedded in other interfaces. This allows you to create a further level of abstraction in your programs for even greater flexibility. Go will automatically identify which struct implements each interface.

It is helpful to understand interface embedding, as many of the Go standard library packages use this technique. For example, the **io** (input/output) package contains a **ReadWriter** interface that embeds **Reader** and **Writer** interfaces, which contain **Read** and **Write** method signatures for reading and writing files.

src\abstr\main.go

94

1 Create two interfaces that each contain two identical method signatures, which all return a string

```
type bird interface {
    speak( ) string
    move( ) string
}

type human interface {
    speak( ) string
    move( ) string
}
```

2 Next, create another interface that embeds the first two interfaces

```
type creature interface {
    bird
    human
}
```

3 Now, add an empty struct and attach methods that satisfy the first (and second) interface

```
type parrot struct{ }

func ( parrot ) speak( ) string {
    return "Squawk, squawk!"
}

func ( parrot ) move( ) string {
    return "A parrot flies away."
}
```

Hot tip

Instances of the **parrot** type will call the methods in Step 3.

...cont'd

4 Now, add another empty struct and attach methods that satisfy the (first and) second interface – and therefore also now satisfies the third interface

```go
type person struct{ }

func ( person ) speak( ) string {
    return "Hi, there!"
}
func ( person ) move( ) string {
    return "A person walks away."
}
```

Instances of the **person** type will call the methods in Step 4.

5 Add a function that receives the third interface as an argument and calls the implemented methods

```go
func nudge( c creature) {
    fmt.Printf( "\n%v \n", c.speak( ) )
    fmt.Printf( "%v \n\n". c.move( ) )
}
```

Method signatures may also specify a parameter list and multiple return types.

6 Add a main function with statements that create instances of each struct, then call their like-named methods

```go
func main( ) {
    var bird1 parrot
    var human1 person
    nudge( bird1 )
    nudge( human1 )
}
```

7 Save the program file in a "abstr" directory, then run the program to see the different outputs

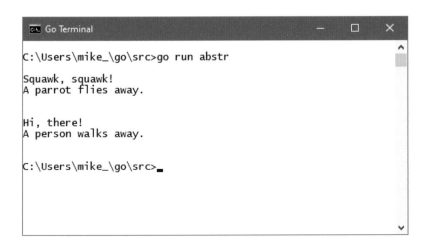

```
C:\Users\mike_\go\src>go run abstr

Squawk, squawk!
A parrot flies away.

Hi, there!
A person walks away.

C:\Users\mike_\go\src>
```

Summary

- Multiple related items of data can be grouped together in a Go **struct** type.

- The **{ }** curly brackets of a **struct** contain a list of name and type pairs that are fields defining what the **struct** will contain.

- An instance of a **struct** can be created as a variable declared with the name of the **struct** as its type.

- An individual field of a **struct** can be initialized by assigning a value to the instance name and dot-suffixed field name.

- An instance of a **struct** can be created and initialized by assigning a **struct** literal to a variable name.

- A function can be attached to a **struct** by adding a receiver, which specifies the **struct** name to the function signature.

- A function attached to a **struct** is referred to as a method.

- A method can be a value receiver, operating on a copy of the **struct**, or a pointer receiver operating on the original fields.

- A **struct** can represent the attributes and behaviors of real-world objects by its field properties and attached methods.

- A **struct** can be embedded inside another **struct** as an anonymous field, so its fields can be directly addressed.

- The three cornerstones of object-oriented programming are encapsulation, inheritance, and polymorphism.

- Encapsulation in Go relies upon data-hiding in packages where only capitalized items will be exported.

- Inheritance in Go relies upon composition where embedded structs provide fields and methods to the embedding **struct**.

- Polymorphism in Go relies upon its **interface** type, which only contains a list of method signatures.

- Any **struct** that has methods that precisely match the **interface** method signatures will implement the **interface**.

- An **interface** can be embedded inside another **interface** to provide further abstraction for additional flexibility.

7 Create Arrays

This chapter demonstrates how to store multiple items of data in indexed elements within a Go program.

Create a Basic Array

An array is a variable that can store multiple items of data – unlike a regular variable, which can only store one piece of data. The pieces of data are stored sequentially in array "elements" that are numbered, starting at zero. So, the first value is stored in element zero, the second value is stored in element one, and so on.

An empty array can be declared using the **var** keyword followed by a name of your choice, followed by [ ] square brackets surrounding an integer specifying the number of required elements. These must then be followed by the data type the elements can contain. The syntax of the declaration looks like this:

var *arrayName* [*nElements*] *dataType*

Values can then be individually assigned to each available element by stating the element number in square brackets:

arrayName [*elementNumber*] *= value*

Alternatively, an array can be declared and initialized with values by stating values for each element in an "array literal" – a comma-separated list, grouped within braces:

arrayName := [*nElements*] *dataType* { *value, value, value* }

Any individual element's value can be referenced using the array name followed by square brackets containing the element number. For example, to reference the value within the first element:

arrayName [**0**]

Collectively, the elements of an array are known as an "index". Arrays can have more than one index – to represent multiple dimensions, rather than the single dimension of a regular array. Multi-dimensional arrays of three indices and more are uncommon, but two-dimensional arrays are useful to store grid-based information, such as coordinates.

To create a two-dimensional array, simply add a second pair of [ ] square brackets specifying the number of required elements, like this:

var *arrayName* [*nElements*] [*nElements*] *dataType*

Values can then be individually assigned to each available element by stating the element numbers in square brackets:

arrayName [*elementNumber*] [*elementNumber*] *= value*

Array numbering starts at zero – so the final element in an array of six elements is number five, not number six. This numbering is known as a "zero-based index".

You can only store data within array elements of the data type specified in the array declaration.

...cont'd

Alternatively, a two-dimensional array can be initialized and values assigned to each element when it is declared by stating values for each index in array literals:

arrayName := [*nElements*] [*nElements*] *dataType*
          { { *value* , *value* , *value* } , { *value* , *value* , *value* } }

Any individual element's value can be referenced using the array name followed by square brackets containing the element numbers for each index. For example, the first element of the second index:

arrayName [0] [1]

1 Create an empty array of three elements that can each only contain string values
var cars [3]string

2 Next, add statements to initialize each array element
cars[0] = "BMW"
cars[1] = "Ford"
cars[2] = "Opel"

3 Now, declare and initialize a two-dimensional array
coords := [2][3]int { { 1, 2, 3 } , { 4, 5, 6 } }

4 Then, add statements to display output containing stored array element values
fmt.Println("Cars:", cars)
fmt.Println("Second Car:", cars[1])
fmt.Println("X1,Y1:", coords[0] [0])
fmt.Println("X2,Y3:", coords[1] [2])

5 Save the program file in a "array" directory, then run the program to see the values stored within array elements

An array in Go programming is of a fixed size – once created, you cannot add or remove elements.

src\array\main.go

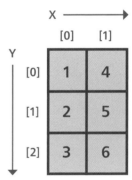

99

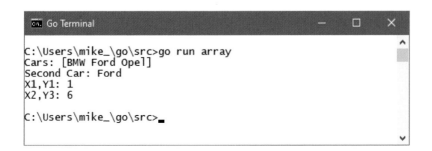

```
Go Terminal                              —   □   ✕

C:\Users\mike_\go\src>go run array
Cars: [BMW Ford Opel]
Second Car: Ford
X1,Y1: 1
X2,Y3: 6

C:\Users\mike_\go\src>_
```

Loop Through Elements

Loops and arrays are perfect partners. A loop can be used to fill each element in an empty array with a value, and can iterate through each element in an array to reference the stored values.

A traditional incrementing **for** loop can set an initial counter variable value at zero, and place that variable within an array variable's [ ] square brackets to represent the index number of each element as the loop proceeds.

Go has a built-in **len( )** function that accepts an array variable as its argument, and returns an integer that is the number of elements contained in the array. This can be used in a traditional **for** loop to exit the loop when it reaches the array's final element.

src\elems\main.go

1 Create an empty integer array of five elements
```
var arr [ 5 ]int
```

2 Next, add a statement to confirm the array size
```
fmt.Println( "No. of Elements:", len( arr ) )
```

3 Now, add a loop to fill each element
```
for i := 0 ; i < len( arr ) ; i++ {
    arr[ i ] = i * i
}
```

4 Then, add a loop to reference each array element value
```
for i := 0 ; i < len( arr ) ; i++ {
    fmt.Printf( "Index: %v Value: %v \n", i, arr[ i ] )
}
```

5 Save the program file in an "elems" directory, then run the program to see the values stored within array elements

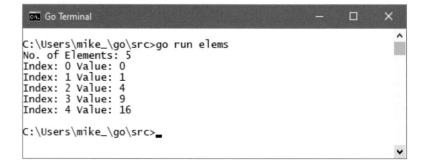

```
C:\Users\mike_\go\src>go run elems
No. of Elements: 5
Index: 0 Value: 0
Index: 1 Value: 1
Index: 2 Value: 4
Index: 3 Value: 9
Index: 4 Value: 16

C:\Users\mike_\go\src>
```

An array index is zero-based, so the final fifth element here is index number 4.

...cont'd

Go provides a couple of special features that you can use with arrays. Firstly, when declaring an array variable with an array literal, you can use the ... wildcard operator to set the number of elements equal to the number of values in the array literal:

arr := [...]int { 10, 20, 30 }   **// len(arr) == 3.**

You can even specify which element each value should be stored in by stating the index number for each value, like this:

arr := [...]int { 2: 10, 0: 20, 1: 30 }   **// arr == [20, 30, 10].**

Secondly, you can use the **range** keyword in a loop to iterate over an array and return the index number and value of each element.

1 Create an integer array of five elements
arr := [...]int { 100, 200, 300, 400, 500 }

2 Next, add a statement to confirm the array size
fmt.Println("No. of Elements:", len(arr))

3 Now, add a loop to modify each element's value
```
for i , v := range arr {
    arr[ i ] =v / 10
}
```

4 Then, add a loop to reference each array element value
```
for i , v := range arr {
    fmt.Printf( "Index: %v Value: %v \n", i, v )
}
```

5 Save the program file in a "range" directory, then run the program to see the values stored within array elements

src\range\main.go

Hot tip

You can replace the variable name **i** with the _ blank identifier to avoid an error if you don't need the index number in the loop statements – see page 68.

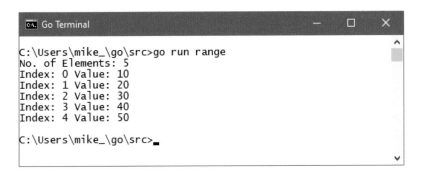

```
C:\Users\mike_\go\src>go run range
No. of Elements: 5
Index: 0 Value: 10
Index: 1 Value: 20
Index: 2 Value: 30
Index: 3 Value: 40
Index: 4 Value: 50

C:\Users\mike_\go\src>
```

Slice Arrays

Arrays are sequences whose elements each contain data of the same type, but are of a fixed length so are not very versatile. Fortunately, Go provides a **slice** type that represents an underlying array and whose length can be changed.

To understand the **slice** type it is important to recognize that a slice does not contain any elements itself, but is merely a reference to an actual array. The **slice** type contains only three components:

- **Ptr** – (pointer) a pointer to the first element in the array accessible by the slice (not necessarily the first array element).

- **Len** – (length) the total number of elements in the slice.

- **Cap** – (capacity) the number of elements between the element referenced by the pointer and the last array element.

For example, a slice of weekdays from an array of day names:

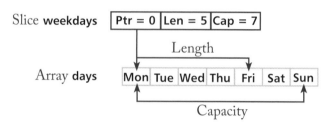

A slice can be created in Go programming by assigning an array to a variable that specifies element index numbers of a desired lower and upper boundary. These are specified around a : colon character between [ ] square brackets. The number to the left of the colon specifies the index number of the starting element to slice – which the slice pointer will reference. The number to the right of the colon specifies the index number of the upper boundary – to slice all elements up to, but not including, the upper boundary element. An assignment for the example depicted above would look like this:

weekdays := days[0 : 5]

Optionally, you can omit either of the numbers that specify the upper and lower boundaries to use the default values. The default value for the lower boundary is 0 (zero) and the default value for the upper boundary is the total number of elements in the array.

Hot tip

Slices are important in Go programming and are seen much more frequently than the array type, but it's important to understand that they are references to underlying arrays.

...cont'd

You can reveal the length of a slice using the built-in **len( )**
function, as with arrays, but you can also check the capacity of a
slice using a built-in **cap( )** function. Comparing the pointer value
of a slice with the memory address of the array element to which
it points, confirms that the slice is indeed a pointer reference.

1 First, create an array of seven elements
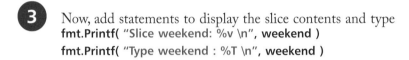

days := **[7]string** {"Mon","Tue","Wed","Thu","Fri","Sat","Sun"}

2 Create a slice that represents the final two array elements
weekend := **days[5 :]**

3 Now, add statements to display the slice contents and type
fmt.Printf("Slice weekend: %v \n", weekend)
fmt.Printf("Type weekend : %T \n", weekend)

4 Add statements to display the slice length and capacity
fmt.Printf("Length weekend: %v \n", len(weekend))
fmt.Printf("Capacity weekend: %v \n", cap(weekend))

5 Finally, add statements to confirm that the slice is a
reference pointing to an underlying array element
fmt.Printf("Pointer weekend: %p \n", weekend)
fmt.Printf("Address days[0]: %p \n", &days[5])

6 Save the program file in a "slice" directory, then run the
program to see the features of a slice

src\slice\main.go

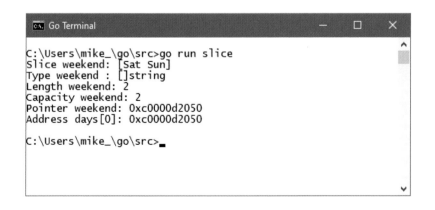

```
Go Terminal                              —   □   ×

C:\Users\mike_\go\src>go run slice
Slice weekend: [Sat Sun]
Type weekend : []string
Length weekend: 2
Capacity weekend: 2
Pointer weekend: 0xc0000d2050
Address days[0]: 0xc0000d2050

C:\Users\mike_\go\src>_
```

Hot tip

See that the type of
a slice is described
by empty [ ] square
brackets followed by the
type each element may
contain.

Make Slices

A slice can be created in the same way as an array, except without specifying any number of elements between [ ] square brackets, and can be initialized with a "slice literal", using this syntax:

sliceName := [ ] *dataType* { *value, value, value* }

You can also create an empty slice using a built-in **make( )** function, whose arguments specify the slice type, slice length, and (optionally) the slice capacity. Values can then be assigned to individual elements, like this:

```
fruitSlice := make( [ ]string , 3 )
fruitSlice[ 0 ] = "Apple"
fruitSlice[ 1 ] = "Banana"
fruitSlice[ 2 ] = "Cherry"
```

In either case, Go will internally create an underlying array of the appropriate length and capacity. You can add elements to a slice using a built-in **append( )** function. This requires at least two arguments that specify the name of the slice and one or more additional element values. The function returns a new slice containing one or more additional elements, like this:

```
fruitSlice = append( fruitSlice, "Damson" )
```

Most importantly, when the length of the enlarged slice exceeds the capacity of the underlying array, Go will automatically increase the capacity of the underlying array to accommodate the elements.

There is also a built-in **copy( )** function that allows you to copy one slice into another. This requires two arguments that specify the name of the slice to copy into, and the name of the slice to copy from. It is useful to create an empty slice of the same length as the source slice, then copy content into it, like this:

```
jamSlice = make( [ ]string , len( fruitSlice ) )
copy( jamSlice, fruitSlice )
```

If you want to remove an element from a slice, and preserve the order of the remaining elements, the **copy( )** function can be used to slide all elements above a specified index number down by one position. Slices can be passed as arguments to functions by specifying a name and the slice type in the function signature.

Don't forget

You need not be unduly concerned about a slice's underlying array, as Go takes care of it automatically.

1 Create an integer slice, initialized by a slice literal
```
nums := [ ]int { 10, 20, 30, 40, 50, 60, 70, 80, 90, 100 }
```

2 Create another slice, then initialize its individual elements
```
more := make( [ ]int, 3 )
more[ 0 ] = 200
more[ 1 ] = 300
more[ 2 ] = 400
```

3 Add a statement that calls a function to describe a slice
```
describe( nums )
```

4 Enlarge the first slice by appending one value from the second slice, then describe the amended first slice
```
nums = append( nums, more[ 0 ] )
describe( nums )
```

5 Remove the first element of the first slice, then describe the amended slice once more
```
copy( nums[ 0 : ], nums[ 1 : ] )
nums = nums[ : len( nums ) - 1 ]
describe( nums )
```

6 After the main function, add the function that describes the first slice's element values, length, and capacity
```
func describe( nums [ ]int ) {
    fmt.Printf( "\n%v Length: %v ", nums, len( nums ) )
    fmt.Printf( "Capacity: %v \n", cap( nums ) )
}
```

7 Save the program file in a "make" directory, then run the program to see the features of a slice

```
C:\Users\mike_\go\src>go run make

[10 20 30 40 50 60 70 80 90 100] Length: 10 Capacity: 10

[10 20 30 40 50 60 70 80 90 100 200] Length: 11 Capacity: 20

[20 30 40 50 60 70 80 90 100 200] Length: 10 Capacity: 20

C:\Users\mike_\go\src>
```

Hot tip

The size of the capacity increment is 10 here, but may vary on other platforms. Notice that the capacity does not resume its original size when the element has been removed.

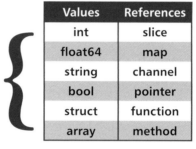

Slices Versus Arrays

An array contains a sequence of values, whereas a slice contains a reference to a sequence of values. This is an important distinction in Go programming that applies to many of its types. Most significantly, when passing a type to a function, those types that are value-based will receive a copy of the original, whereas those types that are references will point to the actual original. In order for the function to operate on an original value, you therefore need to use pointers when passing value-based types to a function, but no pointers are needed when passing references.

Use pointers to change original values from within a function.

{

Values	References
int	slice
float64	map
string	channel
bool	pointer
struct	function
array	method

}

No need to use pointers to change original values from within a function.

Another distinction between arrays and slices concerns "variadic" functions that can be called with any number of arguments. You cannot pass array element values to a variadic function unless you first "convert" the array to a slice by copying the array element values into slice elements.

You can create a variadic function simply by prefixing the final parameter's data type with the ... wildcard operator in the function signature, using this syntax:

func *funcName* (*paramName ...dataType*)

Variadic functions can be called in the usual way, enclosing a comma-separated list of arguments within ( ) parentheses.

Variadic functions are especially useful when passing the values in slice elements to a function, as the length of a slice may change during the execution of a program. Regardless of the length of the slice, its element values can be passed to a variadic function by specifying the slice name followed by the ... wildcard operator, within the parentheses of a function call:

funcName (*sliceName...*)

Hot tip

The **fmt.Printf( )** function is a variadic function – it requires one fixed argument at the beginning, then accepts any number of subsequent arguments.

...cont'd

1 Create an array of three strings
`array := [ 3 ]string{ "BMW", "Ford", "Opel" }`

src\versus\main.go

2 Copy the array elements into a slice to "convert" it
`slice := array[ : ]`

3 Next, call a variadic function to pass the values in each slice element for display
`list( slice... )`

4 Now, append two more values to the slice
`slice = append( slice, "Porsche", "Ferrari" )`

5 Again, call a variadic function to pass the values in each slice element for display
`list( slice... )`

6 After the main function, add the variadic function to list the passed-in values of the slice elements
```
func list( autos ...string ) {
    for i, v := range autos {
        fmt.Printf( "\n%v. %v", i, v )
    }
    fmt.Println( )
}
```

Don't forget

When calling a variadic function, you are not passing the slice itself – you are merely passing the slice element values.

7 Save the program file in a "versus" directory, then run the program to see the parameter values

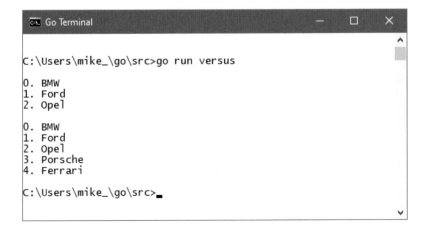

```
C:\Users\mike_\go\src>go run versus

0. BMW
1. Ford
2. Opel

0. BMW
1. Ford
2. Opel
3. Porsche
4. Ferrari

C:\Users\mike_\go\src>
```

Map Keys and Values

Multiple items of data can be stored with associated keys in a hash table, so that you can reference a stored value via its associated key. In Go programming, this data structure is called a "map", but other programming languages call this an associative array or dictionary.

All keys in a map must be unique and be of the same data type. All values in a map must be of the same data type, but not necessarily be of the same data type as the keys.

A map can be created using the **var** and **map** keywords, and by specifying the key and value data types using this syntax:

var *mapName* = **map** [*keyDataType*] *valueDataType*

Individual key/value pairs can then be assigned to the map, like this:

mapName [*"keyName"*] = *value*

Alternatively, you can use the built-in **make( )** function to create a map:

mapName := **make(map** [*keyDataType*] *valueDataType*)

Furthermore, you can create and initialize a map by assigning a "map literal" with this syntax:

mapName := **map** [*keyDataType*] *valueDataType* **{**

       key : *value* , *key* : *value* , *key* : *value* ,

}

Unlike arrays and slices, the key/value pairs are stored in an unordered manner, so you cannot use element index numbers to reference a stored value – you must use its associated key.

You can add key/value pairs to a map at any time, and you can use the built-in **delete( )** function to remove a key/value pair. This requires two arguments to specify the map name and the name of the key that you want to remove.

As with arrays and slices, you can iterate through all the elements of a map using the **range** keyword. In this case, the loop will return the key and value, rather than an index number and value.

A map element is not a variable, so you cannot take its memory address.

...cont'd

1 Create a map for string keys and values
```
colors := make( map [ string ] string )
```

2 Initialize the map with three key/value pairs
```
colors[ "Red" ] = "#FF0000"
colors[ "Green" ] = "#00FF00"
colors[ "Blue" ] = "#0000FF"
```

src\map\main.go

3 Next, display all key/value pairs within the map
```
fmt.Printf( "\nColors: %v \n", colors )
```

4 Now, add a key/value pair and display its value
```
colors[ "Yellow" ] = "#FFFF00"
fmt.Printf( "\nYellow Hex Code: %v \n", colors[ "Yellow" ] )
```

5 Then, remove the added key/value pair
```
delete( colors, "Yellow" )
```

6 Finally, add a loop to list all key/value pairs in the map
```
for k, v := range colors {

    fmt.Printf( "\nHex Code for %v is %v \n", k, v )
}
```

7 Save the program file in a "map" directory, then run the program to see the keys and values

The order of map elements is random and may vary on different platforms.

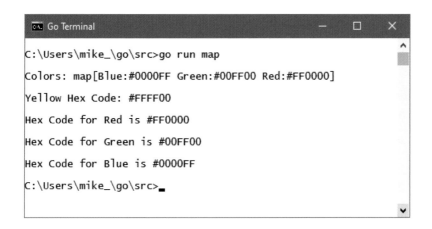

```
Go Terminal                              —   □   ×

C:\Users\mike_\go\src>go run map

Colors: map[Blue:#0000FF Green:#00FF00 Red:#FF0000]

Yellow Hex Code: #FFFF00

Hex Code for Red is #FF0000

Hex Code for Green is #00FF00

Hex Code for Blue is #0000FF

C:\Users\mike_\go\src>_
```

Summary

- An array is a fixed-length structure that stores data sequentially in individual elements.

- An array declaration must specify the number of required elements between [ ] square brackets.

- The data stored in an array or slice element can be referenced by stating the element's index number in [ ] square brackets.

- An empty array can be created using the **var** keyword, or can be created and initialized by assigning an array literal.

- The **len( )** function returns the length of an array or slice.

- The **range** keyword can be used to iterate through elements.

- A slice is a variable-length structure that stores data sequentially in individual elements of an underlying array.

- A slice comprises a pointer, length, and capacity.

- The **cap( )** function returns the capacity of a slice.

- A slice declaration must not specify the number of elements between [ ] square brackets.

- Upper and lower boundaries of a sequence of elements can be specified around a : colon character within [ ] square brackets.

- An empty slice can be created using the **make( )** function, or can be created and initialized by assigning a slice literal.

- Elements can be added to a slice by the **append( )** function.

- A slice can be copied into another slice by the **copy( )** function.

- Pointers are not required when passing references to a function.

- Variadic functions can be called with any number of arguments.

- A map is a variable-length structure containing associated key/value pairs.

- An empty map can be created using the **make( )** function, or can be created and initialized by assigning a map literal.

- The value stored in a map element can be referenced by stating the associated key in [ ] square brackets.

(8) Harness Time

Get Dates

The Go standard library **time** package provides functionality to extract specific fields from a **Time** data type that describe a particular point in time. These can be made available to a program by importing the **time** package.

A date/time instance of a new **Time** data type can be created with fields describing the current date and time using a **time.Now( )** function. The fields are initialized from the system clock on your device for the current locale.

The value within an individual field can be retrieved using an appropriate method of the **Time** data type. For example, the value of the year field can be retrieved using its **Year( )** method. Similarly, there are **Month( )**, **Day( )**, and **Weekday( )** methods that retrieve other individual fields of a **Time** data type.

Method	Returns
Now( )	A **time.Time** data type comprising current date, time, and time zone fields
Year( )	Year with 4 digits (YYYY)
Month( )	Month name of the year
Day( )	Day number of the month
Weekday( )	Day name of the week

There are also these three methods whose returned **Time** data type values can usefully be assigned to variables:

Method	Returns
Date( )	Year with 4 digits (YYYY), month name of the year, and day number of the month
ISOWeek( )	Week number of the year (1-53) and year with 4 digits (YYYY)
YearDay( )	Day number of the year (1-365/366)

The values returned by the **Time** data type methods are not strings.

It is important to recognize that a **Time** data type contains individual fields and so is not a string. You can, however, convert it to a string using its **String( )** method:

1 Begin by importing the Go standard library **time** package into a program

```
import (
    "fmt"
    "time"
)
```

src\date\main.go

2 Next, create a date/time instance of the **Time** data type, initialized with the current date and time

```
dt := time.Now( )
```

3 Add statements to output all fields of the date/time instance and to confirm its data type

```
fmt.Printf( "DateTime: %v \n", dt )
fmt.Printf( "DateTime Type: %T \n", dt )
```

4 Next, add a statement to output today's day name

```
fmt.Printf( "Today is: %v \n", dt.Weekday( ) )
```

5 Now, add statements to display today's date, current week, and day number of the year

```
y, m, d := dt.Date( )
fmt.Printf( "Date: %v %v, %v \n", m, d, y )

yr, wk := dt.ISOWeek( )
fmt.Printf( "Week No.: %v in %v \n", wk, yr )

dy := dt.YearDay( )
fmt.Printf( "Day No.: %v \n", dy )
```

6 Save the program file in a "date" directory, then run the program to see the date field values

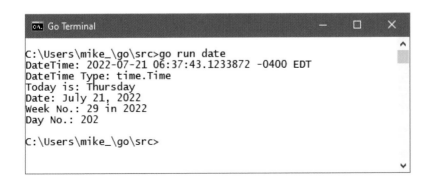

```
Go Terminal                              —  □  ×

C:\Users\mike_\go\src>go run date
DateTime: 2022-07-21 06:37:43.1233872 -0400 EDT
DateTime Type: time.Time
Today is: Thursday
Date: July 21, 2022
Week No.: 29 in 2022
Day No.: 202

C:\Users\mike_\go\src>
```

Hot tip

The time zone values specify the offset from the UTC (Universal Time Clock) and a time zone abbreviation – see page 120 for more on time zones.

Get Times

The time values within individual fields of a **Time** data type can be retrieved using appropriate methods. For example, the value of the hour field can be retrieved using its **Hour( )** method. Similarly, there are **Minute( )**, **Second( )**, and **Nanosecond( )** methods that retrieve other individual fields of a **Time** data type.

Method	Returns
Hour( )	Hour number of the day (0-23)
Minute( )	Minute number of the hour (0-59)
Second( )	Second number of the minute (0-59)
Nanosecond( )	Nanosecond of the second (0-999999999)

Unlike other programming languages, the **time** package in Go does not provide a method to return a millisecond value from a **Time** data type. You can, however, divide the nanosecond value by one million to produce its millisecond equivalent.

There are also these three methods whose returned **Time** data type values can usefully be assigned to variables:

Method	Returns
Clock( )	Hour, minute, and second within the day
Unix( )	The number of seconds elapsed since the epoch (January 1, 1970 00:00:00 UTC)
UnixNano( )	The number of nanoseconds elapsed since the epoch (January 1, 1970 00:00:00 UTC)

The **UnixNano( )** method is useful to seed the Go random number generator – see the example on page 140.

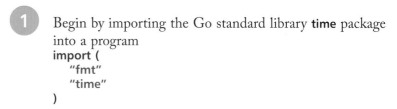

src\times\main.go

1. Begin by importing the Go standard library **time** package into a program
```
import (
    "fmt"
    "time"
)
```

2. Next, create a date/time instance of the **Time** data type, initialized with the current date and time
```
dt := time.Now( )
```

114

3 Add statements to output all fields of the date/time instance and to confirm its data type

```
fmt.Printf( "DateTime: %v \n", dt )
fmt.Printf( "DateTime Type: %T \n\n", dt )
```

4 Next, add statements to evaluate the current hour and display an appropriate greeting

```
hr := dt.Hour( )

switch {
    case hr < 12 :
        fmt.Println( "Good Morning!" )
    case hr < 18 :
        fmt.Println( "Good Afternoon!" )
    default :
        fmt.Println( "Good Evening!" )
}
```

5 Now, add statements to display the current time

```
h, mn, s := dt.Clock( )
fmt.Printf( "Time: %v:%v,:%v \n", h, mn, s )
```

Beware

Single-digit hour, minute, and second values are not returned with a leading zero by default.

6 Finally, add statements to display the current time field for nanoseconds and its equivalent millisecond value

```
ns := dt.UnixNano( )
ms := ns / 1000000

fmt.Println( "Nanoseconds:", ns )
fmt.Println( "Milliseconds:", ms )
```

7 Save the program file in a "times" directory, then run the program to see the time field values

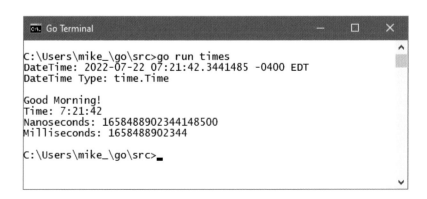

```
Go Terminal                                          —    □    ×

C:\Users\mike_\go\src>go run times
DateTime: 2022-07-22 07:21:42.3441485 -0400 EDT
DateTime Type: time.Time

Good Morning!
Time: 7:21:42
Nanoseconds: 1658488902344148500
Milliseconds: 1658488902344

C:\Users\mike_\go\src>_
```

Format Date and Time

The date and time values within individual fields of a **Time** data type can be formatted in a variety of ways using its **Format( )** method. This takes a single argument that is a "layout" string, which specifies how to format a date/time value. The format must only be specified by exactly using elements of this reference string:

Mon Jan 2 15:04:05 2006 MST

Since **MST** (Mountain Standard Time) is 7 hours behind **UTC** (Universal Time Coordinated), the reference string can alternatively be considered numerically to look like this:

01 02 03:04:05PM '06 -0700

If you want the **Format( )** method to return only the day, month, and time in hh:mm format, the layout can be specified as:

"Mon Jan 2 15:04"

or numerically as:

"01/02 03:04"

You can have the day name and month name returned as full names by specifying the long name versions in the layout:

"Monday January 2 15:04"

The **time** package includes predefined **UnixDate**, **ANSIC**, and **RFC3339** constants that you can use as date/time layout formats.

A custom layout can specify the components in any order to suit different locales – for example, for appropriate date formatting.

The **time** package also includes a predefined **Kitchen** constant that you can use as a time layout format. This will display the time in a 12-hour format and append "AM" or "PM" as appropriate.

Additionally, the time components can be formatted to be displayed in a 24-hour format that will automatically prefix single-digit hours with a zero by specifying **"15:04"**.

Both 12-hour format and 24-hour format will automatically prefix single-digit minutes with a zero.

ANSIC refers to the American National Standards Institute standard date/time format for the C programming language. RFC 3339 refers to the Request For Comment date/time document of the Internet Engineering Taskforce (IETF).

1 Begin by importing the Go standard library **time** package into a program

```
import (
    "fmt"
    "time"
)
```

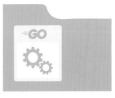

src\format\main.go

2 Next, create a date/time instance of the **Time** data type, initialized with the current date and time, then display its components in various formats

```
dt := time.Now( )
fmt.Println( "\nDefault Format:", dt )
fmt.Println( "Unix Format:", dt.Format( time.UnixDate ) )
fmt.Println( "ANSIC Format:", dt.Format( time.ANSIC ) )
fmt.Println( "RFC3339 Format:", dt.Format( time.RFC3339 ) )
fmt.Println( "Custom Format:",
        dt.Format( "January 2, 2006 [Monday]" ) )
```

3 Now, display only date components formatted to be appropriate in two locales

```
fmt.Println( "\nUS Format:", dt.Format( "January 2, 2006" ) )
fmt.Println( "UK Format:", dt.Format( "2 January, 2006" ) )
```

4 Then, display only time components in a 12-hour format and in a 24-hour format

```
fmt.Println( "\nTime 12-Hour:", dt.Format( time.Kitchen ) )
fmt.Println( "Time 24-Hour:", dt.Format( "15:04" ) )
```

The **time.Kitchen** constant is equivalent to specifying a layout format of "15:04PM".

5 Save the program file in a "format" directory, then run the program to see the formatted date and time field values

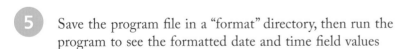

```
Go Terminal                                    —    □    ✕

C:\Users\mike_\go\src>go run format

Default Format: 2022-07-24 14:07:56.0576256 -0400 EDT
Unix format: Sun Jul 24 14:07:56 EDT 2022
ANSIC format: Sun Jul 24 14:07:56 2022
RFC3339 format: 2022-07-24T14:07:56-04:00
Custom Format: July 24, 2022 [Sunday]

US Date Format: July 24, 2022
UK Date Format: 24 July, 2022

Time 12-hour: 2:07PM
Time 24-Hour: 14:07

C:\Users\mike_\go\src>
```

Set Date and Time

You can create your own **Time** data types using the **Date( )** function of the Go standard library **time** package. This requires eight arguments to specify (in this order) a year, a month, a day number, an hour, a minute, a second, a nanosecond, and a location.

All arguments are specified as integer values except for the month and location.

The month can be specified using one of the **time** package predefined full-name month constants for January-December, for example, **time.January**.

The location can be specified using one of the **time** package predefined location constants **time.UTC**, for Universal Time Coordinated or **time.Local**, for your system clock.

The date fields in any **Time** data type can be modified using the **AddDate( )** method of the Go standard library **time** package to specify three arguments for year, month, and day. Positive values will advance the date, and negative values will retard the date. For example, **time.AddDate(1, 0, 0)** will advance the date one year.

Similarly, the **time** package's **Add( )** method can be used to specify a single duration argument by which to modify a date/time. This value can be an **int64** value representing a number of nanoseconds by which to modify the date/time. More conveniently, you can use constants **time.Hour, time.Minute, time.Second,** or **time.Millisecond** to modify individual time fields of a **Time** data type. For example, **time.Add(10 * time.Hour)** will advance the time 10 hours.

You can also create your own **Time** data types from a string using the **Parse( )** function of the Go standard library **time** package. This requires two arguments to specify a layout and a date/time string. Usefully, this function returns two values, which are a **Time** data type and an error. If the function returns a **Time** data type, the error value will be **nil**, otherwise it will be an error message.

The layout should only use values from the Go reference string:

Mon Jan 2 15:04:05 2006 MST

Unless a time zone offset value is specified in the date/time string (e.g. **-0500**), the resulting **Time** data type will assume UTC time.

Don't forget

The **Time** data types can be formatted using the **Format( )** method described on page 116.

1 Begin by importing the Go standard library **time** package into a program

```
import (
    "fmt"
    "time"
)
```

src\setdate\main.go

2 Next, create and display a date/time instance of the **Time** data type, initialized for noon on New Year's day

```
dt := time.Date( 2025, time.January, 1, 12, 0, 0, time.Local )
fmt.Printf( "\nDateTime: %v \n\n", dt )
```

3 Advance the date two years to U.S. Independence Day, then display the modified date

```
dt = dt.AddDate( 2, 6, 3 )
fmt.Printf( "DateTime: %v \n\n", dt )
```

4 Now, initialize a layout string and a date/time string

```
layout := "2006-Jan-02 03:04PM"
str := "2030-Dec-25 12:30AM"
```

Beware

The layout string and date/time string must be in the same format when parsing a string to a **Time** data type.

5 Finally, attempt to create and display the fields of a **Time** data type, or display an error message if the attempt fails

```
t, err := time.Parse( layout, str )
if err != nil {
    fmt.Println( err )
} else {
    fmt.Printf( "Parsed DateTime:" %v \n", t )
}
```

6 Save the program file in a "setdate" directory, then run the program to see the date and time field values

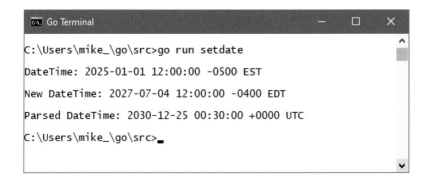

```
Go Terminal                          —   □   ×

C:\Users\mike_\go\src>go run setdate

DateTime: 2025-01-01 12:00:00 -0500 EST

New DateTime: 2027-07-04 12:00:00 -0400 EDT

Parsed DateTime: 2030-12-25 00:30:00 +0000 UTC

C:\Users\mike_\go\src>_
```

Hot tip

The modified **Time** fields automatically recognize the change from Eastern Standard Time to Eastern Daylight Time.

Recognize Zones

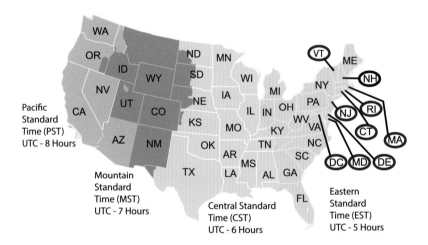

All **Time** data types in Go programming are associated with a time zone. Typically, this will be UTC time, or the local time based upon the location of the system running the program. You can, however, specify an alternative location as an argument to a **time.LoadLocation( )** function. The location name must correspond to a file in the Internet Assigned Numbers Authority (IANA) time zone database, such as "America/New_York", "Asia/Seoul", or "Europe/London". The **time.LoadLocation( )** function returns two values, which are a **Location** type and an error. If the function successfully returns a **Location** type, the error value will be **nil**, otherwise it will be an error message.

You can create a **Time** data type of the current time in another time zone by appending a call to an **In( )** function after its **Now( )** function, in which the location is specified as an argument to the **In( )** function.

Hot tip

A list of IANA location names and TZ abbreviations is included with this book's download files – see page 6.

Hot tip

Daylight Saving in the USA reduces the offset from UTC by one hour. For example, Eastern Daylight Time (EDT) is UTC - 4 hours, Central Daylight Time (CDT) is UTC - 5 hours, etc.

You can ascertain the time zone associated with a **Time** data type by calling its **Zone( )** method. This method returns two values, which are a three-letter TZ time zone abbreviation, such as "EST" (Eastern Standard Time) or "EDT" (Eastern Daylight Time), and a numerical value representing the seconds offset of that time zone from UTC. It is important to note that time zone abbreviations are not unique, so you should not rely solely upon these to recognize particular time zones. Some time zones change their time for Daylight Saving, so you might evaluate both the TZ abbreviation and offset to correctly recognize the time zone.

...cont'd

1 Begin by importing the Go standard library **time** package into a program

```go
import (
    "fmt"
    "time"
)
```

src\zone\main.go

2 Next, create and initialize variables with a default string value and a **Time** data type in a specified location

```go
zone := "All"
loc, _ := time.LoadLocation( "America/New_York" )
dt := time.Now( ).In( loc )
```

A _ blank identifier is used here to ignore the returned error value due to space constraints, but you should ideally include an error-handler.

3 Ascertain the time zone abbreviation and offset seconds, then convert the offset to a positive minute number

```go
abbr, offset := dt.Zone( )
if offset < 1 {
    offset = offset * -1
}
offset /= 60
```

4 Now, evaluate the abbreviation and offset values

```go
switch {
    case abbr == "EST" && offset == 300 :
        zone = "East Coast"
    case abbr == "EDT" && offset == 240 :
        zone = "East Coast"
}
```

5 Display the time zone details and an appropriate message

```go
fmt.Printf( "\nTZ: %v Offset Minutes: %v \n", abbr, offset )
fmt.Println( "Welcome to", zone, "Visitors!" )
```

6 Save the program file in a "zone" directory, then run the program to see the time zone values

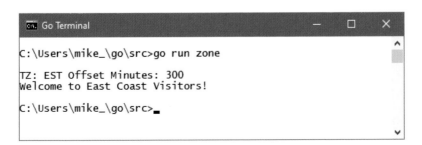

```
Go Terminal                                    —    □    ✕

C:\Users\mike_\go\src>go run zone

TZ: EST Offset Minutes: 300
Welcome to East Coast Visitors!

C:\Users\mike_\go\src>_
```

Delay Time

The Go standard library **time** package provides a **Sleep( )** function that allows you to delay progress of a program by a specified duration period. The duration is supplied as an argument to the **Sleep( )** function, and can be expressed as a multiplication of a **time** package constant. For example, **5 * time.Second** expresses a duration of five seconds.

The Go standard library **time** package also provides three methods that compare an instance of the **Time** data type with another time specified as their argument. These methods will each return a boolean **true** or **false** value according to the result of the time comparison:

Method	Returns
Before(time **)**	A boolean **true** value if the instance time is earlier than its argument time
After(time **)**	A boolean **true** value if the instance time is later than its argument time
Equal(time **)**	A boolean **true** value if the instance time and argument time represent the same instant – even in different time zones

If you would like to see the difference between two instances of the **Time** data type, you can use a **Sub( )** method of a time instance to specify another time instance as its argument. This method will return the elapsed duration between the two instants as an **int64** data type value of nanosecond precision.

It is often preferable to present duration periods with less than nanosecond precision, so the Go standard library **time** package includes a **Round( )** method to specify more concise precision. This method requires one argument to determine your preferred rounding behavior. Typically, the argument is supplied as one of the **time** package constants. For example, calling the method with **Round(time.Millisecond)** will round a nanosecond precision duration to the nearest millisecond, **Round(time.Second)** will round a nanosecond precision duration to the nearest second, and so on.

...cont'd

1 Begin by importing the Go standard library **time** package into a program
```
import (
    "fmt"
    "time"
)
```

src\delay\main.go

2 Next, create and display components of a **Time** data type
```
start := time.Now( )
fmt.Println( "\nStarted At:", start.Format( "03:04:05" ) )
```

3 Now, delay the program's progress for five seconds
```
time.Sleep( 5 * time.Second )
```

4 Then, create and display a second **Time** data type
```
finish := time.Now( )
fmt.Println( "Finished At:", finish.Format( "03:04:05" ) )
```

5 Compare the start and finish times
```
fmt.Println( "\nStart First?:", start.Before( finish ) )
fmt.Println( "Finish First?:", finish.Before( start ) )
```

6 Finally, display the length of the delay
```
diff := finish.Sub( start )
fmt.Println( "\nTime Elapsed:", diff.Round( time.Second ) )
```

7 Save the program file in a "delay" directory, then run the program to see the time delay

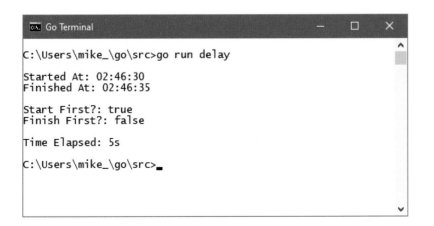

The ability to delay execution is particularly useful in pausing individual "goroutines" – see the example on page 159 for more details.

123

Summary

- The Go standard library **time** package contains functions to create **Time** data types comprising date, time, and zone fields.

- A **Time** data type is not a string, but can be converted to a string using its **String( )** method.

- The **time.Now( )** function returns the current date, time, and zone from the system time at the current locale.

- Date components can be extracted from a **Time** data type using its **Year( )**, **Month( )**, **Day( )**, and **Weekday( )** methods.

- The **Date( )**, **ISOWeek( )**, and **YearDay( )** methods return date values that can usefully be assigned to variables.

- Time components can be extracted from a **Time** data type using **Hour( )**, **Minute( )**, **Second( )**, and **Nanosecond( )** methods.

- The **Clock( )**, **Unix( )**, and **UnixNano( )** methods return time values that can usefully be assigned to variables.

- The **Format( )** method takes a layout string or predefined constant as its argument to format dates and times.

- The Go reference string for date/time layouts is **Mon Jan 2 15:04:05 2006 MST**

- The **time.Date( )** function is used to create a **Time** data type and requires arguments to specify year, month, day, hour, minute, second, nanosecond, and location.

- The **time** package contains predefined constants for month names, hour, minute, second, millisecond, and location.

- The **AddDate( )** method can modify date components and the **Add( )** method can modify time components.

- The **time.LoadLocation( )** function requires an IANA location name argument, and the **In( )** function applies a location.

- The **time.Sleep( )** function delays execution of a program by the duration specified as its argument.

- The **Sub( )** method returns elapsed duration between two times, and the **Round( )** method can specify its precision.

9 Manage Data

Unite Strings

In Go programming, a **string** is zero or more characters enclosed within double quote marks. So, these are all valid **string** values:

s1 := "My First String"

s2 := ""

s3 := "2"

s4 = "nil"

The empty quotes of **s2** initialize the variable as an empty **string** value. The numeric value assigned to **s3** is a **string** representation of the number. The Go **nil** zero value, which normally represents the absence of any value, is simply a **string** literal when it is enclosed within quotes.

Essentially, a **string** is a collection of characters; each character containing its own data – just like elements in a defined array. It is, therefore, logical to regard a **string** as an array of characters and apply array characteristics when dealing with **string** values. The built-in **len( )** function will return the number of characters in a **string**, much like it returns the number of elements in an array.

The + operator, which can be used to add numeric values, doubles as a concatenation operator for joining **string** values together to create a single united string.

The Go standard library **strings** package contains useful functions for string manipulation. Its **Join( )** function joins (concatenates) all elements of a string array to create a single united string. This function requires two arguments to specify the name of a string array and a separator value to be placed between each string element in the united string. Typically, you will specify a single space as the separator to create a space-separated united string.

The **fmt.Printf( )** and **fmt.Println( )** functions that write to standard output can add spaces and newline characters to output, but do not change the actual strings. They do, however, both return two values, which are the number of bytes written and any write error. If no error is encountered, the error value will be **nil** as usual. With the English language, the number of bytes written will normally represent the number of characters output – including non-printing characters contained within the string.

Hot tip

The ASCII code number for a non-printing **\t** tab character is 9, and for a non-printing **\n** newline character is 10.

1 Begin by importing the Go standard library **strings** package into a program

```
import (
    "fmt"
    "strings"
)
```

src\join\main.go

2 Initialize two string variables and a concatenated string

```
s1, s2 := "The Truth is rarely Pure ", "and never Simple."
str := s1 + s2
```

3 Next, output the concatenated string and its length

```
chars, err := fmt.Printf( "\n%v \n", str )
if err != nil {
    fmt.Println( err )
} else {
    fmt.Println( "Bytes Written: ", chars )
    fmt.Println( "String Length:", len( str ) )
}
```

4 Initialize a string array and a joined string

```
arr := [ ]string { "\n\tStrive", "For", "Greatness!" }
ast := strings.Join( arr, " " )
```

5 Now, output the joined string and first two characters

```
fmt.Println( ast )
if ast[ 0 ] == 10 && ast[ 1 ] == 9 {
    fmt.Printf( "1st Char: ASCII %v Newline\n", ast[ 0 ] )
    fmt.Printf( "2nd Char: ASCII %v Tab\n", ast[ 1 ] )
}
```

6 Save the program file in a "join" directory, then run the program to see the united strings

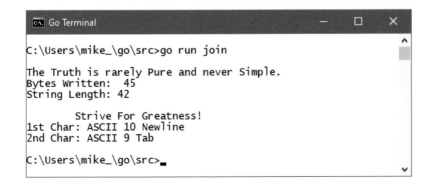

```
C:\Users\mike_\go\src>go run join

The Truth is rarely Pure and never Simple.
Bytes Written:  45
String Length: 42

        Strive For Greatness!
1st Char: ASCII 10 Newline
2nd Char: ASCII 9 Tab

C:\Users\mike_\go\src>
```

Don't forget

The number of bytes written here exceeds the string length because the **fmt.Printf( )** method adds two newline characters and one space character.

Split Strings

The Go standard library **strings** package provides several functions that allow a specified string to be separated into substrings. These functions treat the string like an array in which each element contains a character or a space.

Frequently, you may want to separate a space-separated sentence into an array of substrings that are each individual words. The **strings** package conveniently provides a **Fields( )** function that will perform that very task. This function requires the string sentence as its sole argument, and will return an array of substrings containing each individual word from that string.

The **strings** package has a **Split( )** function that requires two arguments to specify a string and a separator. This function will return an array of substrings that exist between occurrences of the specified separator. For example, when the string is a space-separated sentence and the separator is a space character, the **Split( )** function will return an array of words within that sentence.

The **strings** package also has a **SplitN( )** function that works just like the **Split( )** function, but accepts a third argument to specify how many substrings to return. Subsequent occurrences of the specified separator will simply be returned in the final substring if the specified number of substrings exceeds the number of separators. For example, when the string is a space-separated sentence, the separator is a space character, and only two substrings are specified, the **SplitN( )** function will return a substring containing the first word in the sentence and a substring containing the entire remainder of that sentence including spaces.

It is important to recognize that the **Fields( )**, the **Split( )**, and the **SplitN( )** functions discard the specified separator and only include the characters around the separator in the returned substrings. There are, however, two further functions that allow you to also include the separators in the returned substrings.

The **strings** package's **SplitAfter( )** function works like the **Split( )** function, but includes the separator in the returned substrings. Similarly, the **strings** package's **SplitAfterN( )** function works like the **SplitN( )** function, but includes the separator in the returned substrings.

Hot tip

Data is often stored as Comma-Separated Values in CSV files, which can be usefully split into individual values.

1 Begin by importing the Go standard library **strings** package into a program

```
import (
    "fmt"
    "strings"
)
```

src\split\main.go

2 Start the main function by initializing a string variable

```
str := "I can, and, I will."
```

3 Next, add statements to pass a description and substrings of the variable string to a listing function

```
list( "Fields", strings.Fields( str ) )

list( "Split", strings.Split( str, "," ) )
list( "SplitN", strings.SplitN( str, ",", 2 ) )

list( "SplitAfter", strings.SplitAfter( str, "," ) )
list( "SplitAfterN", strings.SplitAfterN( str, ",", 2 ) )
```

4 After the main function, add the function to list the description and all substrings upon each call

```
func list( desc string, subs [ ]string ) {
    fmt.Print( "\n", desc, ": " )
    for _, v := range subs {
        fmt.Print( "[", v, "] " )
    }
    fmt.Print( "\n" )
}
```

5 Save the program file in a "split" directory, then run the program to see the substrings

```
Go Terminal                                    —   □   X

C:\Users\mike_\go\src>go run split

Fields: [I] [can,] [and,] [I] [will.]

Split: [I can] [ and] [ I will.]

SplitN: [I can] [ and, I will.]

SplitAfter: [I can,] [ and,] [ I will.]

SplitAfterN: [I can,] [ and, I will.]

C:\Users\mike_\go\src>_
```

Don't forget

Only split methods that contain the word "After" in their name will retain the separators.

Find Characters

The Go standard library **strings** package provides several functions that allow a specified string to be searched to find a specified character or substring (pattern). These functions treat the string as an array in which each element contains a character or a space.

The **strings** package has a **Contains( )** function that requires two arguments to specify a string and a pattern to find. This function will simply return **true** or **false** to indicate the result of a (case-sensitive) search. For example, to search for a "Pro" pattern:

strings.Contains("Go Programming in easy steps", "Pro")

The **strings** package also has an **Index( )** function that requires two arguments to specify a string and a pattern to find. This function will return an integer that is the index position of the first instance of the pattern in the searched string if the search succeeds, otherwise it will return -1 when the search fails.

The **strings** package's **Count( )** function requires two arguments to specify a string and a pattern to find. You can use this function to discover how many non-overlapping instances of a pattern occur in a searched string. If the pattern is an empty string, this function will normally return 1 plus the number of characters in the searched string. This allows you to determine the number of characters in a searched string by deducting 1 from the returned integer.

The **strings** package's **HasPrefix( )** function requires two arguments to specify a string and a pattern to find. This function will return **true** or **false** to indicate whether the searched string begins with the specified pattern.

Similarly, the **strings** package's **HasSuffix( )** function requires two arguments to specify a string and a pattern to find, and will return **true** or **false** to indicate whether the searched string ends with the specified pattern.

You can modify a searched string by replacing a specified pattern with a replacement substring using the **strings** package's **Replace( )** function. This function requires four arguments to specify the string to search, the pattern to find, the replacement substring, and an integer denoting the number of instances to be replaced. If you want to replace all instances of the pattern within the searched string, simply specify -1 as the number of replacements.

The **strings.Index( )** function stops searching when it finds the first instance of the pattern in the searched string.

1 Begin by importing the Go standard library **strings** package into a program

```
import (
    "fmt"
    "strings"
)
```

src\find\main.go

2 Start the main function by initializing a string variable

```
str := "I can resist everything except temptation"
```

3 Next, test whether a substring exists within the string, then find the index position of the first instance

```
fmt.Printf( "\nFound 'an': %v \n", strings.Contains( str, "an" ) )
fmt.Printf( "Found 'an' at: %v \n", strings.Index( str, "an" ) )
```

4 Now, count how many instances of a particular letter appear in the string

```
fmt.Printf( "Count of 'e': %v \n", strings.Count( str, "e" ) )
```

5 Then, test whether the string begins or ends with a particular substring

```
fmt.Printf( "Prefix 'ion': %v \n", strings.HasPrefix( str, "ion" ) )
fmt.Printf( "Suffix 'ion': %v \n", strings.HasSuffix( str, "ion" ) )
```

6 Finally, replace a substring within the string

```
fmt.Println( strings.Replace( str, "temptation", "chocolate", 1 ) )
```

7 Save the program file in a "find" directory, then run the program to see the search results

```
C:\Users\mike_\go\src>go run find

Found 'an': true
Found 'an' at: 3
Count of 'e': 6
Prefix 'ion': false
Suffix 'ion': true
I can resist everything except chocolate

C:\Users\mike_\go\src>
```

Convert Strings

The Go standard library **strings** package provides functions to convert the character case of strings.

The **strings** package has a **ToUpper( )** function that requires a single string argument. This function will simply return a copy of the string with all its characters converted to uppercase letters.

Similarly, the **strings** package's **ToLower( )** function requires a single string argument, and will return a copy of the string with all its characters converted to lowercase letters.

The **strings** package also has a **ToTitle( )** function that requires a single string argument. This function will return a copy of the string with the first character of each word converted to an uppercase letter – but only when the string argument is all lowercase. If you want to convert a string of mixed-case letters to title case you must first convert it to lowercase using the **strings** package's **ToLower( )** function.

When a program receives user input following a request for a numeric value, the input might be of a **string** data type and may include spaces that the user has inadvertently entered. You can remove spaces from the beginning and end of a string using the **strings** package's **Trim( )** function. This requires two arguments to specify the string and character to be removed. To remove all leading and trailing spaces, the second argument will be " " to specify a single space character.

Once unnecessary spaces have been removed from a string containing an input number, the data type must be converted to a numeric type before the program can use the input in arithmetical operations. This can be achieved by importing the Go standard library **strconv** package. This package contains an **Atoi( )** function (ASCII to Integer) that requires a single string argument, and will return an integer and any error. If no error is encountered, the error value will be **nil** or it will contain a descriptive error message if the method cannot return an integer data type.

Similarly, the **strconv** package contains an **Itoa( )** function that can convert an integer to a string data type. This method simply requires an integer argument, and will return a string copy.

132

A **strconv.ParseInt( )** method can also be used to convert a string data type to an integer. The **strconv.Atoi( )** method is equivalent to calling **strconv.ParseInt(str, 10, 0)**.

...cont'd

1 Begin by importing the Go standard library **strings** package and **strconv** package into a program
```
import (
    "fmt"
    "strings"
    "strconv"
)
```

src\conv\main.go

2 Start the main function by initializing a string variable, then display the string with different character cases
```
str := "I have Nothing to declare except My Genius"
fmt.Println( strings.ToUpper( str ) )
fmt.Println( strings.ToLower( str ) )
fmt.Println( strings.Title( strings.ToLower( str ) ) )
```

3 Now, assign a number and spaces to the variable
```
str = "  42  "
fmt.Printf( "\n%v Type: %T, Length: %v \n", str, str, len( str ) )
```

Hot tip

4 Then, remove leading and trailing spaces from the string
```
str = strings.Trim( str, " " )
fmt.Printf( "\n%v Type: %T, Length: %v \n", str, str, len( str ) )
```

Change the string assignment to " $42 " in Step 3, then save and run the program to see a parsing error message appear as the conversion to an integer fails.

5 Finally, attempt to change the data type to an integer
```
num, err := strconv.Atoi( str )
if err != nil {
    fmt.Println( err )
} else {
    fmt.Printf( "%v Type: %T \n", num, num )
}
```

6 Save the program file in a "conv" directory, then run the program to see the string conversions

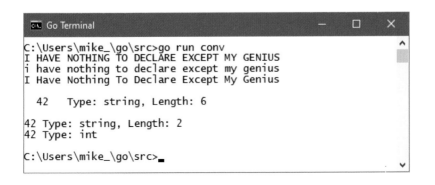

Calculate Areas

The Go standard library **math** package provides a number of useful functions and constant mathematical values. The constants are listed in the table below together with their approximate value:

Constant	Description
math.E	Constant e, base of the natural logarithm, with an approximate value of 2.71828
math.Pi	The constant π Pi, with an approximate value of 3.14159
math.Phi	The constant φ Phi (the "Golden Ratio"), with an approximate value of 1.61803
math.Sqrt2	The square root of 2, with an approximate value of 1.41421
math.SqrtE	The square root of constant e, with an approximate value of 1.64872
math.SqrtPi	The square root of constant π Pi, with an approximate value of 1.77246
math.SqrtPhi	The square root of constant φ Phi, with an approximate value of 1.27202
math.Ln2	The natural logarithm of 2, with an approximate value of 0.69315
math.Log2E	The base-2 logarithm of constant e, with an approximate value of 1.44269
math.Ln10	The natural logarithm of 10, with an approximate value of 2.30259
math.Log10E	The base-10 logarithm of constant e, with an approximate value of 0.43429

Hot tip

The Golden Ratio appears many times in geometry and art. It is the ratio of a line segment cut into two pieces of different lengths, where the length ratio of the long piece to the short piece is equal to the length ratio of the whole segment to the long piece.

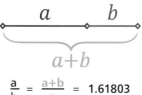

$$\frac{a}{b} = \frac{a+b}{a} = 1.61803$$

The **math** constants are mostly used in Go programs that have a particular mathematical purpose, but all the **math** package constants are listed above for completeness.

...cont'd

1 Begin by importing the Go standard library **math** package into a program

```
import (
    "fmt"
    "math"
)
```

src\area\main.go

2 Declare three floating-point variables

```
var rad, area, perim float64
```

3 Next, initialize the first variable and display its value to two decimal places

```
rad = 4
fmt.Printf( "\nRadius of Circle: %.2f \n", rad )
```

4 Now, calculate the area of a circle based on the given radius, then display the area to two decimal places

```
area = math.Pi * ( rad * rad )
fmt.Printf( "\nArea of Circle: %.2f \n", area )
```

5 Then, calculate the perimeter of a circle based on the given radius, and display the perimeter to two decimal places

```
perim = 2 * ( math.Pi * rad )
fmt.Printf( "\nPerimeter of Circle: %.2f \n", perim )
```

6 Save the program file in an "area" directory, then run the program to see the calculated values

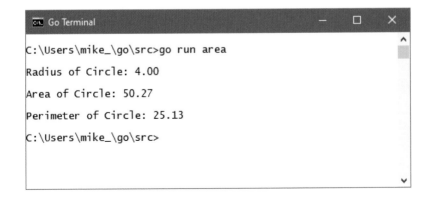

Don't forget

Refer back to page 24 for more on formatting decimal places in output.

Evaluate Numbers

The Go **math** package provides these useful functions that can be used to evaluate **float64** arguments:

Function	Returns
math.Abs( )	An absolute value
math.Acos( )	An arc cosine value
math.Asin( )	An arc sine value
math.Atan( )	An arc tangent value
math.Atan2( )	An angle from an X-axis point
math.Ceil( )	A rounded-up value
math.Cos( )	A cosine value
math.Exp( )	An exponent of constant e
math.Floor( )	A rounded-down value
math.IsNaN( )	A boolean **true** or **false** value
math.Log( )	A natural logarithm value
math.Max( )	The larger of two numbers
math.Min( )	The smaller of two numbers
math.Pow( )	A power value
math.Round( )	The nearest integer value
math.Sin( )	A sine value
math.Sqrt( )	A square root value
math.Tan( )	A tangent value

Hot tip

The **math.IsNan( )** function (Is-Not-a-number) is useful to discover whether a value cast to the **float64** data type is indeed a number.

Hot tip

The **math** package contains lots more functions but those listed here are useful for many mathematical operations. Discover more in the Go documentation at **golang.org/pkg/math**

...cont'd

1 Begin by importing the Go standard library **math** package into a program
```go
import (
   "fmt"
   "math"
)
```

src\maxmin\main.go

2 Next, initialize two variables
```go
square := math.Pow( 5, 2 )      // 5 to power 2 ( 5 x 5 ).
cube := math.Pow( 4, 3 )        // 4 to power 3 ( 4 x 4 x 4 ).
```

3 Now, compare the positive value of the variables and display the largest and smallest numbers
```go
fmt.Println( "\nLargest Positive:", math.Max( square, cube ) )
fmt.Println( "\nSmallest Positive:", math.Min( square, cube ) )
```

4 Then, add statements to reverse the numerical polarity of each variable – making positive values into negative values
```go
square *= -1
cube *= -1
```

5 Finally, compare the negative value of the variables and display the largest and smallest numbers
```go
fmt.Println( "\nLargest Negative:", math.Max( square, cube ) )
fmt.Println( "\nSmallest Negative:", math.Min( square, cube ) )
```

6 Save the program file in a "maxmin" directory, then run the program to see the compared values

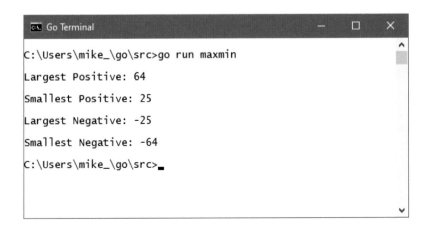

```
Go Terminal                                  —  □  ×

C:\Users\mike_\go\src>go run maxmin

Largest Positive: 64

Smallest Positive: 25

Largest Negative: -25

Smallest Negative: -64

C:\Users\mike_\go\src>_
```

Don't forget

The largest negative value is the one closest to zero.

Round Decimals

The Go standard library **math** package provides a number of useful functions for rounding a decimal value to a near integer. These functions are listed in the table below, together with a brief description of each one:

Function	Returns
math.Floor(x)	The greatest integer less than x
math.Ceil(x)	The least integer greater than x
math.Round(x)	The nearest integer to x
math.Trunc(x)	The integer part of x

Hot tip

The **math.Round( )** function will round up from the mid-point, so **math.Round(7.5)** returns **8**, not **7**.

If you want to reduce a long floating-point value to just two decimal places, first multiply the floating-point value by 100, then use **math.Round( )** to remove any remaining decimal places, then divide by 100 to return two decimal places.

Procedures that multiply, operate, then divide can be written as individual steps, or parentheses can be used to determine the order in a single succinct expression. For example, commuting a long floating point value in a variable named "num" can be written as:

```
num = num * 100
num = math.Round( num )
num = num / 100
```

or alternatively as:

```
num = math.Round( num * 100 ) / 100
```

The Go programming language has a strong type system that unlike other programming languages, does not support type conversion (a.k.a. "casting") implicitly. You can, however, perform explicit type conversion between compatible data types, such as **float64** and **int** types using the syntax *dataType(value)* to convert a value to another data type. In converting a floating-point value to an integer, the value is truncated, losing the decimal places.

1 Begin by importing the Go standard library **math** package into a program
```
import (
   "fmt"
   "math"
)
```

src\round\main.go

2 Initialize a floating-point variable and display its value
```
var pi float64 = math.Pi
fmt.Println( "Pi:", pi )
```

3 Next, display nearest integers to the floating-point value
```
fmt.Println( "\nFloor:", math.Floor( pi ) )
fmt.Println( "Ceiling:", math.Ceil( pi ) )
fmt.Println( "Round:", math.Round( pi ) )
fmt.Println( "Truncated:", math.Trunc( pi ) )
```

4 Now, reduce the floating-point value to two places
```
fmt.Println( "\nShort Pi:", math.Round( pi * 100 ) / 100 )
```

5 Finally, initialize another floating-point variable and cast its value to an integer variable
```
var e1 float64 = math.E
fmt.Printf( "\nE: %v %T \n", e1, e1 )
var e2 int = int( e1 )
fmt.Printf( "Cast: %v %T \n", e2, e2 )
```

6 Save the program file in a "round" directory, then run the program to see the rounded decimals

```
Go Terminal                              —   □   ×

C:\Users\mike_\go\src>go run round
Pi: 3.141592653589793

Floor: 3
Ceiling: 4
Round: 3
Truncated: 3

Short Pi: 3.14

E: 2.718281828459045 float64
Cast: 2 int

C:\Users\mike_\go\src>_
```

Generate Randoms

The Go standard library **math** package contains a **rand** package that provides functions to generate pseudo-random numbers. You can make this available to your program by importing **math/rand**.

The **rand.Intn( )** function returns a random number from zero up to the number specified as its argument. The **rand.Perm( )** function returns a sequence of integers, from zero up to the number specified as its argument, in a pseudo-random order.

The randomizing pattern is based upon a default "seed" that will return the same pseudo-random order each time the program runs. This may be what you want, but often it is preferable to generate a different order each time the program runs. To make this happen, you must specify a custom seed as an integer argument to a **rand.Seed( )** function that will be unique each time the program runs. It is convenient to use the current system time for this purpose by calling the **time.Now( )** function and extracting the integer count of elapsed nanoseconds since the Epoch using the **Time** data type's **UnixNano( )** method. This value will be different each time the program runs, so specifying this integer as the argument to the **rand.Seed( )** function will ensure a different pseudo-random order is generated each time the program runs.

Hot tip

In computing, the Epoch is the time at midnight on January 1, 1970.

140

src\lotto\main.go

1 Import the Go standard library **math/rand** package into a program, along with the **time** package to set a random seed and the **strconv** package to convert random numbers

```
import (
    "fmt"
    "math/rand"
    "strconv"
    "time"
)
```

2 Next, specify a unique seed for the random generator
```
rand.Seed( time.Now( ).UnixNano( ) )
```

3 Now, generate a slice of integers from zero to 58
```
nums := rand.Perm( 59 )
```

4 Then, increment the range to become 1-59 inclusive
```
for i := 0 ; i < len( nums ) ; i++ {
    nums[ i ]++
}
```

5 Assign the first six numbers in pseudo-random order around hyphen characters in a formatted string
```
str := "\nYour Six Lucky Numbers: "
for i := 0 ; i < 6 ; i++ {
    str += strconv.Itoa( nums[ i ] )
    if i != 5 {
        str += " - "
    }
}
```

The **int** numbers must be converted to the **string** data type for concatenation.

6 Finally, display the formatted string
```
fmt.Println( str )
```

7 Save the program file in a "lotto" directory, then run the program repeatedly to see different random numbers

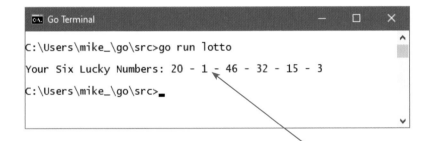

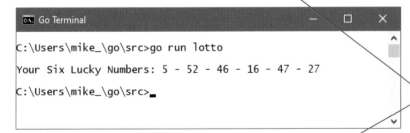

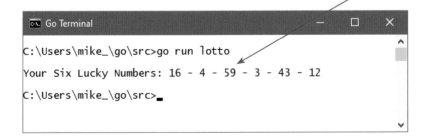

Here the random numbers are in the range 1 to 59 – to play the UK Lotto game or the US New York Lotto game.

Summary

- A **string** is a collection of characters, like elements in an array.

- The built-in **len( )** function returns the number of characters in a **string** specified as its argument.

- The **strings** package contains functions for string manipulation, such as the **Join( )** concatenation function.

- The **Fields( )** and **Split( )** functions each return an array of substrings from a specified **string** argument.

- The **Contains( )** and **Index( )** functions can be used to find a specified substring in a **string** argument.

- The **Count( )** function reports how many instances of a substring occur in a specified **string** argument.

- The **HasPrefix( )** and **HasSuffix( )** functions can be used to recognize the beginning and end of a **string** argument.

- The **Replace( )** function can substitute a substring.

- Character case can be changed using the **ToUpper( )**, **ToLower( )**, and **ToTitle( )** functions.

- The **Trim( )** function can remove leading and trailing spaces.

- The **strconv** package contains **Atoi( )** and **Itoa( )** functions that can convert between **string** and **int** data types.

- The **math** package contains mathematical functions, such as **math.Pow( )**, and mathematical constants, such as **math.Pi**.

- Decimal values can be rounded to near integers using **math.Floor( )**, **math.Ceil( )**, **math.Round( )**, and **math.Trunc( )**.

- The **math/rand** package provides functions to generate pseudo-random numbers.

- The **rand.Perm( )** function returns a randomized sequence of integers from zero up to the number specified as its argument.

- The **rand.Seed( )** function can specify a custom seed integer for the random number generator.

- A unique random seed can be specified each time a program runs by calling the **time.Now( ).UnixNano( )** functions.

10 Handle Input

Get User Input

The previous examples have illustrated how variables can be used to store text string values, numeric integer and floating-point decimal values, and boolean truth values in your programs. Now, they can be used to create a Guessing Game program by storing a generated random integer whose value the user will have to guess, a boolean truth value that will end the game when the user guesses correctly, and a variable containing the user's guess.

The familiar Go standard library **fmt** package provides **Scan( )**, **ScanIn( )**, and **Scanf( )** functions to read from standard input:

- **fmt.Scan( )** stores successive space-separated values into successive interface variables, and regards newlines as spaces.

- **fmt.ScanIn( )** stores successive space-separated values into successive interface variables until it meets a newline.

- **fmt.Scanf( )** stores successive space-separated values into successive interface variables using a specified format.

Each of these functions returns two values, which are the number of items scanned and any read error. If no error is encountered, the error value will be **nil** as usual. Each function also requires one or more arguments to specify the address of interface variables.

The Guessing Game program can use the **fmt.Scan( )** function to assign an input integer guess to an interface variable and compare its value against a generated random integer.

src\scan\main.go

1. Begin by importing the Go standard library **math/rand** and **time** packages into a program, to provide a custom seeded random number generator
   ```
   import (
       "fmt"
       "math/rand"
       "time"
   )
   ```

2. Now, begin the main function by seeding the random number generator with the current time
   ```
   rand.Seed( time.Now( ).UnixNano( ) )
   ```

...cont'd

3 Next, declare and initialize three variables
```
var num int = rand.Intn( 20 ) + 1
var guess int = 0
var flag bool = true
```

4 Then, request the user enter an integer
```
fmt.Print( "\nGuess My Number 1-20: " )
```

5 Finally, add a loop to repeatedly compare the input against the random number until they match
```
for flag {
    _, err := fmt.Scan( &guess )

    if err != nil {
        fmt.Println( err )
    } else if guess > num {
        fmt.Print( "Too High, Try Again: " )
    } else if guess < num {
        fmt.Print( "Too Low, Try Again: " )
    } else if guess == num {
        fmt.Println( "Correct - My Number Is", num )
        flag = false
    }
}
```

Notice that the _ blank identifier is used to ignore the returned number of items scanned, and remember to use the & address of operator when assigning the input values to the interface variables.

6 Save the program file in a "scan" directory, then run the program to guess the randomly generated number

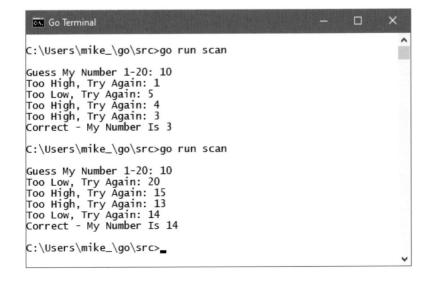

```
C:\Users\mike_\go\src>go run scan

Guess My Number 1-20: 10
Too High, Try Again: 1
Too Low, Try Again: 5
Too High, Try Again: 4
Too High, Try Again: 3
Correct - My Number Is 3

C:\Users\mike_\go\src>go run scan

Guess My Number 1-20: 10
Too Low, Try Again: 20
Too High, Try Again: 15
Too High, Try Again: 13
Too Low, Try Again: 14
Correct - My Number Is 14

C:\Users\mike_\go\src>_
```

Buffer Input

When you want to gather larger items of data into your program it is often preferable to store the data stream in a memory buffer. The Go standard library **bufio** (buffered input/output) package provides a **Scanner** type, which is a memory buffer with several useful methods to handle data streams. You can make this available to your program by importing the **bufio** package.

A **Scanner** instance is first created by specifying a source from which to read data as an argument to the **bufio** package's **NewScanner( )** function. When the source is to be user input, you can import the Go standard library **os** package and specify **os.Stdin** (standard input) as the argument to **NewScanner( )**.

The **Scanner** instance has a **Scan( )** method that reads all the user input and a **Text( )** method that returns the input that has been read as a single **string** value.

The **Scanner** instance also has an **Err( )** method that will return any read error. If no error is encountered, the error value will be **nil** as usual. It is useful to check for errors after calling the **Scan( )** method and **Text( )** method.

If you want to separate the input into individual string items, you can import the Go standard library **strings** package and specify the input to its **Fields( )** function, to split the string into words.

src\buffer\main.go

1 Begin by importing the Go standard library **bufio**, **os**, and **strings** packages into a program, to handle input
```
import (
    "fmt"
    "bufio"
    "os"
    "strings"
)
```

2 Next, request user input
```
fmt.Print( "\nEnter Text:" )
```

3 Now, create a **Scanner** instance to store the user input in a memory buffer, then read the user input
```
scanner := bufio.NewScanner( os.Stdin )
scanner.Scan( )
```

...cont'd

4 Then, output an error if one occurred or the stored data
```
if scanner.Err( ) != nil {
    fmt.Println( scanner.Err( ) )
} else {
    fmt.Println( scanner.Text( ) )
}
```

The **if** conditional test is made as the **Scan( )** method returns a boolean **true** value while reading input, but returns **false** when it reaches the end on input.

5 Next, create a new **Scanner** instance to store other user input in a memory buffer
```
fmt.Print( "\nEnter Text:" )
scanner = bufio.NewScanner( os.Stdin )
scanner.Scan( )
```

6 Then, store individual items of the user input in individual elements of a slice
```
words := strings.Fields( scanner.Text( ) )
```

7 Finally, output an error if one occurred, or list the individual items of user input
```
if scanner.Err( ) != nil {
    fmt.Println( scanner.Err( ) )
} else {
    for i, v := range words {
        fmt.Printf( "%v: %v \n", i, v )
    }
}
```

8 Save the program file in a "buffer" directory, then run the program to see the user input

```
Go Terminal                                    —   □   ×

C:\Users\mike_\go>go run buffer

Enter Text:C++ Programming in easy steps
C++ Programming in easy steps

Enter Text:Go Programming in easy steps
0: Go
1: Programming
2: in
3: easy
4: steps

C:\Users\mike_\go>
```

Command Flags

The command to run your program can recognize any number of parameters, so you can pass a space-separated list of argument values to the program when you run it. The Go standard library **os** (operating system) package provides an **Args** slice, which stores these argument values in individual elements. You can make this available to your program by importing the **os** package.

It is important to note that the very first element in **os.Args** will always contain the path to your program – argument values are then stored sequentially in subsequent elements. You can reference the argument values using [ ] square brackets as you would with any other slice – for example, the first argument value as **os.Args[1]**.

src\params\main.go

1. Begin by importing the Go standard library **os** package into a program, to store command-line arguments
```
import (
    "fmt"
    "os"
)
```

2. Next, add a loop to display the program's default location on your system, together with any passed-in arguments
```
for i, v := range os.Args {
    fmt.Printf( "Argument %v: %v \n", i, v )
}
```

3. Now, display the final passed-in argument
```
fmt.Println( "\nLast Argument:", os.Args[ len( os.Args )-1 ] )
```

4. Save the program file in a "params" directory, then run the program with command-line arguments to see the output

Hot tip

Run **go build params** to compile the program, then run it with the command **params a b c** to see the local program path instead of its default system location.

```
Go Terminal                                          —    □    ×

C:\Users\mike_\go>go run params a b c
Argument 0: C:\Users\mike_\AppData\Local\Temp\exe\params.exe
Argument 1: a
Argument 2: b
Argument 3: c

Last Argument: c

C:\Users\mike_\go>
```

148

The Go standard library **flag** package provides functions for more advanced command-line processing. You can make these available to your program by importing the **flag** package.

You define flags using the **flag** package's **String( )**, **Int( )**, or **Bool( )** functions. These each require three arguments to specify a flag name, default value, and a help message for that flag. They return the address of an appropriate variable data type to store the value. The user can optionally specify an alternative value for each flag at the command-line, prefixing the flag name with a hyphen. The **flag** package's **Parse( )** function applies the user's values to the flag.

1. Begin by importing the Go standard library **flag** package into a program, to parse command-line flags
```
import (
    "fmt"
    "flag"
)
```

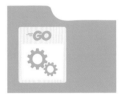

src\flags\main.go

2. Next, define three command-line flags
```
txt := flag.String( "txt", "C#", "A string" )
num := flag.Int( "num", 8, "An integer" )
sta := flag.Bool( "sta", false, "A boolean" )
```

3. Now, process the flags and display their values
```
flag.Parse( )
fmt.Println ( "\nText:", *txt )
fmt.Println( "Number:", *num, " Status:", *sta )
```

4. Save the program file in a "flags" directory, then run the program without and with input to see the flag values

You need to use the * dereference operator to reference the value stored at the address of each defined flag.

```
Go Terminal                              —   □   ×

C:\Users\mike_\go>go run flags

Text: C#
Number: 8  Status: false

C:\Users\mike_\go>go run flags -txt=Go -num=42 -sta=true

Text: Go
Number: 42  Status: true

C:\Users\mike_\go>_
```

Read Files

The Go standard library **io** package contains an **ioutil** (input/output utility) package that provides functions to read text files. You make this available to your program by importing **io/ioutil**.

The **ioutil** package's **ReadFile( )** function takes the path to a text file as its argument, and returns the entire text file content and any read error. If no error is encountered, the error value will be **nil**. It is good practice to check for errors after each file operation.

For finer control when reading text files, you can specify the path to a text file as an argument to the **os** package's **Open( )** function. This simply opens the text file, for reading only, and returns an **os.File** type and any read error. The file type has **Read( )**, **Seek( )**, and **Close( )** methods that allow you to process the text file's content.

The **Seek( )** method determines the position at which to begin reading from the opened file. It requires two arguments to specify an offset position number and a zero (**0**) if this is relative to the start of the file, or one (**1**) if it is relative to the current position.

The **Read( )** method requires a **byte** slice argument whose length will determine the number of bytes (characters) to read from the specified position. This method returns the number of bytes read and any read error.

The **Close( )** method needs no arguments but must be called after completing other operations on an opened file. So that this requirement is not forgotten, you can call the **Close( )** method with the **defer** keyword immediately after opening a file. This will then automatically close the file at the end of the enclosing function.

src\read\main.go

1. Begin by importing the Go standard library **ioutil** and **os** packages into a program, to read a text file
```
import (
    "fmt"
    "io/ioutil"
    "os"
)
```

2. Next, add a function to check for read errors
```
func check( err error ) {
    if err != nil {
        fmt.Println( err )
    }
}
```

...cont'd

3 Now, in the main function, read an entire text file, then check for errors and display the text content
```
txt, err := ioutil.ReadFile( "C:/Textfiles/Oscar.txt" )
check( err )
fmt.Println( string( txt ) )
```

4 Next, open the same text file, then check for errors and remember to close the file after other operations complete
```
file, err := os.Open( "C:/Textfiles/Oscar.txt" )
check( err )
defer file.Close( )
```

5 Then, specify a starting position and check for errors
```
pos, err := file.Seek( 42, 0 )
check( err )
```

6 Now, read 15 characters and check for errors
```
slice := make( [ ]byte, 15 )
nb, err := file.Read( slice )
check( err )
```

7 Finally, display the starting position, the number of characters read, and the text that has been read
```
fmt.Printf( "\n%v bytes @ %v: ", nb, pos )
fmt.Printf( "%v\n", string( slice[ : nb ] ) )
```

8 Save the program file in a "read" directory, then run the program to see the text read from the specified file

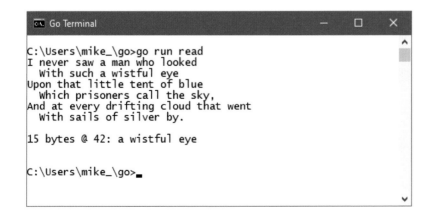

Hot tip

The text file **Oscar.txt** is included in the download archive of examples in this book (see page 6), but you will need to adjust the path in these steps to suit its location on your system.

Don't forget

You have to use the **string( )** function to translate the **byte** slice character code numbers into their respective alphabetic characters.

Write Files

The Go standard library **io** package contains an **ioutil** (input/output utility) package that provides functions to write text files. You make this available to your program by importing **io/ioutil**.

The **ioutil** package's **WriteFile( )** function takes three arguments to specify the path to the file to be written, a **byte** slice of text characters to be written, and the numerical file permissions of that file. This function returns an error message if the attempt to write fails, or an error value of **nil** if the file gets successfully written.

For finer control when writing text files, you can use the **os** package's **OpenFile( )** function. This requires three arguments to specify the path of the file to be written, a flag specifying the operation type, and the numerical file permissions of that file. The flags specifying the operation type are **os** package constants. For example: **os.O_RDWR** to read and write, **os.O_APPEND** to append text, or **os.O_CREATE** to create a new file if none exists.

The **OpenFile( )** function returns an **os.File** type and any read error. The file type has **Write( )** and **Close( )** methods that allow you to process the text file's content.

The **Write( )** method requires a **byte** slice argument containing the text to be written. This method returns the number of bytes read and any read error.

The **Close( )** method can be called with the **defer** keyword immediately after opening a file, to close the file at the end of the enclosing function after the file operations complete.

Hot tip

There are several operation type flags, and multiple flags can be specified to the **OpenFile( )** function. For more details, refer to the documentation at golang.org/pkg/os/#OpenFile

src\write\main.go

1 Begin by importing the Go standard library **ioutil** and **os** packages into a program, to write a text file

```
import (
    "fmt"
    "io/ioutil"
    "os"
)
```

2 Next, add a function to check for write errors

```
func check( err error ) {
    if err != nil {
        fmt.Println( err )
    }
}
```

3 Now, in the main function, write an entire text file, then check for errors

```
txt := [ ]byte( "\nA thousand suns will stream on thee,
                \nA thousand moons will quiver.\n" )
err := ioutil.WriteFile( "C:/Textfiles/Farewell.txt", txt, 0644 )
check( err )
```

4 Next, open the same text file for an append operation, then check for errors and remember to close the file

```
file, err := os.OpenFile( "C:/Textfiles/Farewell.txt",
                          os.O_APPEND, 0644 )
check( err )
defer file.Close( )
```

5 Now, append text to the existing file content and check for errors

```
slice := [ ]byte( "by Alfred Lord Tennyson.\n" )
nb, err := file.Write( slice )
check( err )
```

6 Finally, display the number of characters written, and the text that has been written

```
fmt.Printf( "\nAppended: %v bytes - %v",
                          nb, string( slice[ : nb ] ) )
```

7 Save the program file in a "write" directory and run the program to write the text, then display the file contents

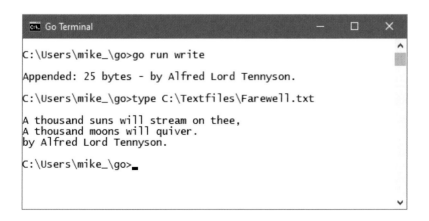

Hot tip

The last three digits in the permission represent Owner, Group, and Other users respectively. Each may have file permission to execute (1 point), write (2 points), and read (4 points). Totaling these points with **0644** allows the Owner to read and write to the file, but Group and Other users may only read the file. This protects the file from unauthorized changes.

Hot tip

A file type also has a **WriteString( )** method that works just like the **Write( )** method but accepts a **string** argument, rather than a **byte** slice argument.

Use Temporary Files

It is sometimes useful to create a temporary file on the user's system in which to store data during the execution of a Go program. The Go standard library **io** package has the **ioutil** package containing a **TempFile( )** function for this purpose.

The **TempFile( )** function returns an **os.File** type, and an error message or **nil** if the file gets created. This function requires two arguments to specify the directory in which to create the file and a filename pattern. You can specify the directory as a path, or as an "" empty string if you are happy to create the temporary file in the system's default directory for temporary files. You specify the file name pattern simply as a name string to which a generated random string will be appended. If the pattern includes a * wildcard character, the generated string will replace that character.

When the **TempFile( )** function successfully creates a temporary file, it automatically opens that file ready to write and read. The returned file type has a **Name( )** method with which to reference its path, including the pattern and random string file name. You can employ its **Write( )** and **WriteString( )** methods to add text content, and use its **Close( )** method when processing is complete. As with other text files, the temporary file's content can be read using the **ioutil.ReadFile( )** function.

You can delete a temporary file when it is no longer required by specifying its file name as the argument to an **os.Remove( )** function. You can also examine the temporary file (and other files) by specifying a file name as the argument to the **os.Stat( )** function. This returns an info type, plus an error message or **nil**.

src\temp\main.go

① Begin by importing the Go standard library **ioutil** and **os** packages into a program, to process a temporary file
```
import (
    "fmt"
    "io/ioutil"
    "os"
)
```

② Next, add a function to check for errors
```
func check( err error ) {
    if err != nil {
        fmt.Println( err )
    }
}
```

3 Now, in the main function, create a temporary text file, then check for errors and confirm the file exists
```
tmpFile, err := ioutil.TempFile( "", "Data-*" )
check( err )
fmt.Printf( "\nCreated File:\n%v \n", tmpFile.Name( ) )
```

4 Write text into the temporary file, then check for errors
```
nb, err := tmpFile.WriteString( "Go Programming Fun!\n" )
check(err)
```

5 Next, read text from the temporary file and check for errors, then display the number of characters read
```
txt, err := ioutil.ReadFile( tmpFile.Name( ) )
check( err )
fmt.Printf( "\nRead: %v bytes - %v \n", nb, string( txt ) )
```

6 Remember to close the file after processing completes
```
tmpFile.Close( )
```

7 Then, delete the temporary file
```
os.Remove( tmpFile.Name( ) )
```

8 Finally, attempt to examine the (now removed) temporary file and check for errors
```
_, err = os.Stat( tmpFile.Name( ) )
check( err )
```

The _ blank identifier represents the info type that is not used in this program.

9 Save the program file in a "temp" directory, and run the program to create, write, read, and delete a temporary file

```
C:\Users\mike_\go>go run temp

Created File:
C:\Users\mike_\AppData\Local\Temp\Data-875527451

Read: 20 bytes - Go Programming Fun!

CreateFile C:\Users\mike_\AppData\Local\Temp\Data-875527451:
The system cannot find the file specified.

C:\Users\mike_\go>_
```

Summary

- The Go standard library **fmt** package provides **Scan( )**, **ScanIn( )**, and **Scanf( )** functions to read from standard input.

- The **Scan( )**, **ScanIn( )**, and **Scanf( )** functions each return two values of the number of items scanned and any read error.

- If no error is encountered when reading from standard input, the returned error value will be **nil**.

- The Go standard library **bufio** package provides a **Scanner** type, which is a memory buffer for data streams.

- A **Scanner** has a **Scan( )** method to read input, a **Text( )** method to return text, and an **Err( )** method to return errors.

- The Go standard library **strings** package provides a **Fields( )** function that can split a string into individual words.

- The Go standard library **os** package provides an **Args** slice, which stores command-line argument values in elements.

- The Go standard library **flag** package has **String( )**, **Int( )**, and **Bool( )** functions that each specify a flag name, default value, and a help message.

- The **flag** package's **Parse( )** function applies the user's values to a flag.

- The Go standard library **io** package contains an **ioutil** package that provides a **ReadFile( )** function to read an entire text file.

- The Go standard library **os** package has **Open( )**, **Read( )**, **Seek( )**, and **Close( )** methods to process a text file's content.

- The **Close( )** method can be called with the **defer** keyword to close a file later, after all file operations complete.

- The Go standard library **io/ioutil** package provides a **TempFile( )** function to create temporary files.

- The **TempFile( )** function returns an **os.File** type that has **Name( )**, **Write( )**, **WriteString( )**, and **Close( )** methods to add content to a temporary file.

- The **os.Remove( )** function can delete files, and the **os.Stat( )** function can examine file information.

11 Employ Concurrency

Create Goroutines

Go programs, like those written in other programming languages, generally execute their code line-by-line in a sequential manner. But Go programming also supports "goroutines" that provide the ability for lines of code to be executed concurrently, side-by-side. This is a big reason why many people choose Go programming.

Concurrency provides the potential to take advantage of multi-core processors, but it is important to distinguish the difference between concurrency and parallelism:

- **Parallelism** is when two tasks are performed at exactly the same time. For example, on a multi-core processor when one core is performing a task and another core is performing a different task – simultaneously. This, however, is difficult to achieve with program code that is executed line-by-line.

- **Concurrency** is the separation of program code into independently-executing tasks that could potentially run simultaneously and produce a correct final result. So a concurrent program is one that can be parallelized. Goroutines provide this ability in Go program code.

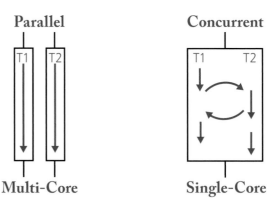

Goroutines are lightweight threads that can execute concurrently. A sequential program with multiple function calls will execute each function in turn, but a concurrent program with goroutines allows multiple functions to be active at the same time.

A goroutine is created by inserting the **go** keyword before an ordinary function call or method call. The order in which tasks are executed is determined internally by the Go scheduler.

1 Begin by importing the Go standard library **time** package into a program, to allow delay for a goroutine to execute
```
import (
    "fmt"
    "time"
)
```

src\goroutine\main.go

2 Add a function containing a loop to print the iteration number and a string argument at 1-second intervals
```
func count( item string ) {
    for i := 1 ; i <= 3 ; i++ {
        fmt.Printf( "%v %v   ", i, item )
        time.Sleep( 1 * time.Second )
    }
    fmt.Println( )
}
```

3 Now, in the main function, add ordinary function calls to execute sequentially
```
fmt.Println( "\nLine-by-Line Execution..." )
count( "moose" )
count( "sheep" )
```

You can also start goroutines from self-invoking functions.

4 Then, in the main function, add a goroutine and an ordinary function call to execute concurrently
```
fmt.Println( "\nConcurrent Execution..." )
go count( "moose" )
count( "sheep" )
```

5 Save the program file in a "goroutine" directory, then run the program to see the differing output

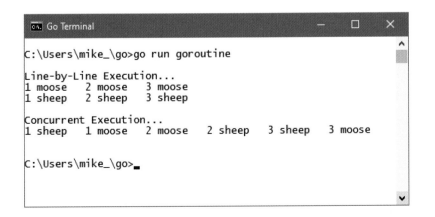

```
Go Terminal                                       —   □   ×

C:\Users\mike_\go>go run goroutine

Line-by-Line Execution...
1 moose    2 moose    3 moose
1 sheep    2 sheep    3 sheep

Concurrent Execution...
1 sheep    1 moose    2 moose    2 sheep    3 sheep    3 moose


C:\Users\mike_\go>_
```

By default, a program will exit when the main goroutine completes – regardless of whether there are any other goroutines that have yet to complete.

Keep Waiting

Go programs might often include multiple goroutines, so the Go standard library **sync** package provides a **WaitGroup** type that can be used to wait for a collection of goroutines to finish execution.

An instance of a **WaitGroup** is created in the usual way, as a variable with this syntax:

var *waitgroupName* **sync.WaitGroup**

The **WaitGroup** is simply a counter that can keep a total of the number of running goroutines. It has these methods that you use to block the program until all the goroutines have completed:

- **Add( )** – Increments the **WaitGroup** counter by the number specified as its argument. For each new goroutine added to the program, the counter should be increased by one.

- **Done( )** – Decrements the **WaitGroup** counter by one automatically, so no argument is required. The counter should by decreased by one when each goroutine completes.

- **Wait( )** – Blocks the program until the **WaitGroup** counter reaches zero, so no argument is required. When the final running goroutine decrements the counter to zero, blocking is automatically removed.

When passing a **WaitGroup** as an argument to a function, it must be passed as a pointer. This means that the argument will specify its memory address, using the **&** address-of operator, and the function parameter will denote it as a pointer using the * prefix operator. The receiving function can then call the **Done( )** method of the **WaitGroup** using the pointer argument.

The **Add( )** method should be called to increment the **WaitGroup** counter before the statement that actually creates the goroutine.

Optionally, the **Add( )** method argument can specify the total number of goroutines in a collection, rather than incrementing each added goroutine to the **WaitGroup** counter individually.

You can reuse a **WaitGroup** to control execution of a subsequent collection of goroutines, but you can only call the **Add( )** method for these after the **Wait( )** method for the previous collection has reached zero.

The order in which goroutines get executed is controlled by the Go scheduler, and can vary each time the program runs.

1 Begin by importing the Go standard library **sync** and **time** packages, to wait for goroutines and to allow a delay

```
import (
    "fmt"
    "sync"
    "time"
)
```

src\waitgroup\main.go

2 Next, in the main function, create a **WaitGroup** instance

```
var wg sync.WaitGroup
```

3 Now, add a loop to increment the counter and pass the address of the **WaitGroup** as a function argument

```
for i := 1 ; i <= 3 ; i++ {
    wg.Add( 1 )
    go report ( i, &wg )
}
```

4 Finally, in the main function, block until the **WaitGroup** counter reaches zero

```
wg.Wait( )
```

5 Now, add a function to confirm the start and end of each goroutine, then notify the **WaitGroup** to stop waiting

```
func report( i int, wg *sync.WaitGroup) {
    fmt.Printf( "\nGoroutine %v Started", i )
    time.Sleep( 1 * time.Second )
    fmt.Printf( "\n\t\t\tGoroutine %v Ended", i )
    wg.Done( )
}
```

Hot tip

You could instead use **defer wg.Done( )** at the start of the function to ensure the Waitgroup gets notified of completion.

6 Save the program file in a "waitgroup" directory, then run the program to see the program wait for the goroutines

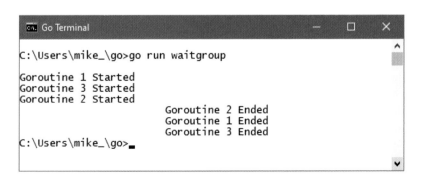

```
Go Terminal                              —  □  ×

C:\Users\mike_\go>go run waitgroup

Goroutine 1 Started
Goroutine 3 Started
Goroutine 2 Started
                    Goroutine 2 Ended
                    Goroutine 1 Ended
                    Goroutine 3 Ended
C:\Users\mike_\go>
```

Make Channels

Goroutines allow code to be executed concurrently in an independent manner, but you can enable goroutines to communicate with each other by the use of "channels".

A Go channel is like a pipe through which you can send a message or receive a message. It is important to recognize that the sending and receiving actions are "blocking" operations – when sending a message, the channel will wait until the receiver is ready to accept the message, and when receiving a message, the channel will wait until the sender actually delivers the message.

Channels are created by specifying the **chan** keyword and a data type as arguments to the built-in **make( )** function, like this:

channelName := **make(chan** *dataType* **)**

You can send a value to the channel using an **<-** arrow operator to direct a value into the channel, with this syntax:

channelName **<-** *message*

Conversely, you can receive a value from a channel using the **<-** arrow operator to direct a value into a variable, with this syntax:

variableName **<-** *channelName*

It is important to ensure that a receiver is not left waiting for a message that will never arrive. This would cause a fatal error called "deadlock" – where the program can never proceed. To avoid this situation, the sender can specify the channel name as an argument to a built-in **close( )** function to explicitly close the channel when it will not send any more messages.

The receiver can, optionally, receive a second value that is a boolean that is **true** when the channel is open, and **false** when the channel is closed.

variableName, channelOpenState **<-** *channelName*

This can be used to examine the channel state, and is useful to exit a loop containing a receiver after a channel has definitely closed.

Beware

Only a sender should close a channel – never use a receiver to close a channel in case the sender hasn't finished.

...cont'd

1 Begin by importing the Go standard library **time** package, to allow a delay and get a current time

```
import (
    "fmt"
    "time"
)
```

src\channel\main.go

2 Next, in the main function, create a channel for strings

```
c := make( chan string )
```

3 Add a goroutine that passes a string value and channel

```
go count( "Message", c )
```

4 Now, add a loop containing a channel receiver that will print received messages until the channel gets closed

```
for {
    msg, open := <- c
    if !open {
        break
    }
    fmt.Println( msg )
}
```

5 Now, add the function with a loop containing a channel sender that will send messages at 1-second intervals, then close the channel when the loop ends

```
func count( msg string, c chan string ) {
    for i := 0; i < 3; i++ {
        c <- msg + " at " + time.Now( ).Format( "04:05" )
        time.Sleep( 1 * time.Second )
    }
    close( c )
}
```

Hot tip

You can refer back to pages 116-117 for more on time formatting.

6 Save the program file in a "channel" directory, then run the program to see the channel messages

```
C:\Users\mike_\go>go run channel
Message at 40:15
Message at 40:16
Message at 40:17

C:\Users\mike_\go>
```

Buffer Channels

Channels are, by default, "unbuffered". This means that you can only send a message into the channel if there exists a corresponding receiver to which the message can be delivered.

As the message sending action is a blocking operation, the message may not be deliverable to a corresponding receiver unless the sender is in a separate goroutine from the receiver.

If the receiver is simply listed within the same function block, the blocking action of the sender will prevent the program progressing to the receiver – so deadlock will occur:

src\unbuf\main.go

1 Begin a main function by creating a channel for strings
`c := make( chan string )`

2 Next, send a message to the channel
`c <- "Go Programming"`

3 Now, add a receiver and output the message
`msg := <- c`
`fmt.Println( msg )`

4 Save the program file in an "unbuf" directory, then run the program to see a fatal error deadlock message

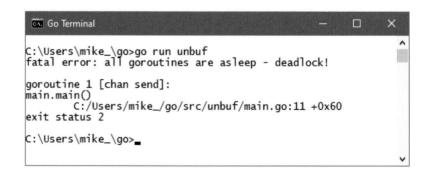

The sender in Step 2 blocks, so the program never reaches the receiver in Step 3.

You can overcome this limitation by including a second argument to the built-in **make( )** function, to specify a buffer size. This allows you to send multiple items to the channel as a queue, and it will only block when the buffer capacity is exceeded.

The **range** keyword can be used in a loop to receive each channel item until the channel gets closed.

1 Begin a main function by creating a channel for strings, with an arbitrary buffer capacity for 10 string items
```
c := make( chan string, 10 )
```

2 Next, send one message to the channel
```
c <- "Go Programming"
```

3 Now, add a receiver and output the message
```
msg := <- c
fmt.Printf( "\n%v \n\n", msg )
```

4 Then, send several messages to the channel
```
c <- "Go Programming"
c <- "in "
c <- "easy "
c <- "steps"
```

5 Now, close the channel after all the messages have been sent to the channel
```
close( c )
```

6 Add a loop that receives and prints each message sent to the channel
```
for msg := range c {
    fmt.Println( msg )
}
```

Hot tip

You can choose any buffer size – but deadlock will occur if the chosen size is exceeded.

7 Save the program file in a "chanbuf" directory, then run the program to see the messages sent and received

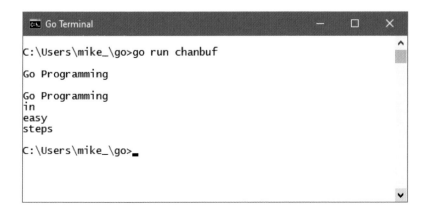

```
C:\Users\mike_\go>go run chanbuf

Go Programming

Go Programming
in
easy
steps

C:\Users\mike_\go>
```

Select Channels

When multiple goroutines send messages to channels at different times, the program may block progress while waiting to receive messages from the slower channels. Go provides a solution to this blocking action by simultaneously listening for messages from multiple channels in a **select** statement block. This has similar syntax to the **switch** statement described on page 50, but a **select** statement blocks until one of its **case** statements finds a match. When a match is found, the statements associated with that **case** statement get executed. This ability to combine goroutines and channels is a powerful feature of the Go programming language.

To continuously listen for channel messages, a **select** statement can be enclosed inside an infinite **for** loop. The loop can be exited by including a **case** statement with an associated statement that will **break** out of the loop to an outer label.

The Go standard library **time** package provides a useful **After( )** function that can be used to create a "timeout" to limit execution time of the listening loop. This requires a duration period as its argument, and returns a channel of the **time.Time** type – that will be the future time after the duration beyond the current time. Testing for when the current time matches the timeout channel with a **case** statement can be used to exit a listening loop.

src\select\main.go

1 Begin by importing the Go standard library **time** package, to wait for goroutines and to create a timeout
```
import (
    "fmt"
    "time"
)
```

2 Next, in the main function, create a timeout channel and two empty channels
```
c0 := time.After( 7 * time.Second )
c1 := make( chan string )
c2 := make( chan string )
```

3 Now, add two goroutine calls that each pass a channel
```
go fastCount( c1 )
go slowCount( c2 )
```

...cont'd

4 After the main function, add the two called functions that will send channel messages at different intervals

```go
func fastCount( c1 chan string ) {
    for {
        time.Sleep( 1 * time.Second )
        c1 <- time.Now( ).Format( "04:05" )
    }
}

func slowCount( c2 chan string ) {
    for {
        time.Sleep( 2 * time.Second )
        c2 <- time.Now( ).Format( "04:05" )
    }
}
```

5 Now, back in the main function, add an infinite loop to receive messages from any of the three channels

```go
Listener:
    for {
        select {
        case done := <- c0 :
            fmt.Println( "Timed Out at ", done.Format( "04:05" ) )
            break Listener
        case msg1 := <- c1 :
            fmt.Println( "1-Second Message at ", msg1 )
        case msg2 := <- c2 :
            fmt.Println( "\t\t\t\t2-Second Message at ", msg2 )
        }
    }
```

An unlabeled **break** statement would only break out of the **select** statement – allowing the **for** loop to continue! A labeled **break** statement breaks out of both the **select** statement and the infinite **for** loop.

6 Save the program file in a "select" directory, then run the program to see the channel messages

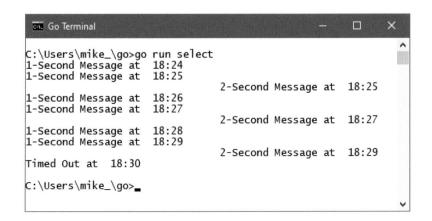

Synchronize Goroutines

The blocking action of unbuffered channels, where the sending action blocks a sending goroutine until another goroutine receives the delivery on the same channel, causes the sending and receiving goroutines to synchronize. In fact, unbuffered channels are sometimes referred to as "synchronous channels".

Channels can, therefore, be used to connect goroutines together in a "pipeline", in which an item sent from one goroutine is the item received by another goroutine. Each goroutine in the pipeline will wait until the channel has been "drained" before sending the next item along the pipeline.

By default, channels can both send and receive, but when you pass a channel to a goroutine you can specify in the function parameter whether the channel may only send items, or only receive items. A send-only channel is specified in the parameter by prefixing the **chan** keyword with the **<-** arrow operator, like this:

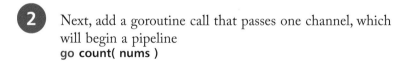
func *funcName* (*paramName* **<-chan** *dataType*)

Conversely, a receive-only channel is specified in the parameter by suffixing the **chan** keyword with the **<-** arrow operator, like this:

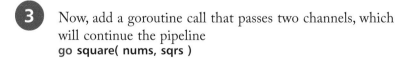
func *funcName* (*paramName* **chan<-** *dataType*)

Specifying a single permissible direction is recommended to reduce the possibility of bugs in your programs.

src\synchronize\main.go

1 Begin a main function by creating two unbuffered channels for integer items
nums := make(chan int)
sqrs := make(chan int)

2 Next, add a goroutine call that passes one channel, which will begin a pipeline
go count(nums)

3 Now, add a goroutine call that passes two channels, which will continue the pipeline
go square(nums, sqrs)

4 After the main function, add the first called function, with a receive-only channel to which it will send 10 individual integers one-by-one when the pipeline is clear

```
func count( nums chan<- int ) {
    for i := 1 ; i <= 10 ; i++ {
        nums <- i
    }
    close( nums )
}
```

5 Add the second called function with a send-only channel, and a receive-only channel to which it will send 10 individual results one-by-one when the pipeline is clear

```
func square( nums <-chan int, sqrs chan<- int ) {
    for i := 1 ; i <= 10 ; i++ {
        num := <- nums
        sqrs <- num * num
    }
    close( sqrs )
}
```

Hot tip

If the sender knows that no further values will be sent to the receiving channel, it can usefully close that channel.

6 Now, back in the main function, add a loop to receive the results at the end of the pipeline

```
for i := 1 ; i <= 10 ; i++ {
    num := <- sqrs
    fmt.Printf( "%v x %v = %v \n", i, i, num )
}
```

7 Save the program file in a "synchronize" directory, then run the program to see the pipeline results

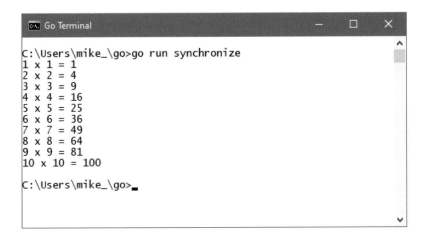

```
C:\Users\mike_\go>go run synchronize
1 x 1 = 1
2 x 2 = 4
3 x 3 = 9
4 x 4 = 16
5 x 5 = 25
6 x 6 = 36
7 x 7 = 49
8 x 8 = 64
9 x 9 = 81
10 x 10 = 100

C:\Users\mike_\go>_
```

Use Worker Pools

If your program has a queue of tasks to perform where the order in which the results are produced is not important, you can employ a "worker pool" – using goroutines and channels.

A worker pool lets you send tasks from multiple concurrent calls to a goroutine that completes each task in a random order determined by the Go scheduler. You can use a **WaitGroup** to wait for the multiple goroutines to complete, or simply send the task results to nothing – to drain the channel and ensure that all worker goroutines have finished.

Task Queue

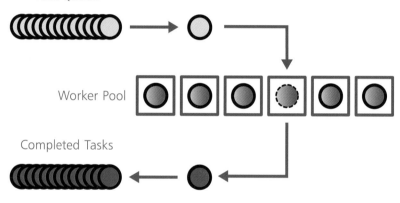

Worker Pool

Completed Tasks

src\workers\main.go

① Begin by importing the Go standard library **time** package, to delay a worker goroutine function
```
import (
    "fmt"
    "time"
)
```

② Next, in the main function, initialize a jobs total number variable, and create two buffered channels of the total size
```
numJobs := 10
jobs := make( chan int, numJobs )
results := make( chan int, numJobs )
```

③ Now, add three worker goroutine calls that each pass an ID number and the two channels
```
go worker( 1, jobs, results )
go worker( 2, jobs, results )
go worker( 3, jobs, results )
```

4 Send an integer for each of 10 jobs, then close that channel to indicate that is all the jobs in the queue

```
for i := 1 ; i <= numJobs ; i++ {
    jobs <- i
}
close( jobs )
```

5 After the main function, add the called worker function that accepts the worker ID number, has a send-only channel from which to receive the job numbers, and a receive-only channel to which it will send 10 results

```
func worker( id int, jobs <-chan int, results chan<- int ) {
    for job := range jobs {
        fmt.Print( "Worker ", id, " ran Job ", job )
        fmt.Printf( " ...%v x %v = %v \n", job, job, job*job )
        time.Sleep( 1 * time.Second )
        results <- job
    }
}
```

Hot tip

The 1-second delay in this example merely simulates the time taken to perform a more lengthy task.

6 Now, back in the main function, add a loop to collect the results and ensure that all the workers have completed

```
for i := 1 ; i <= numJobs ; i++ {
    <- results
}
close( results )
```

7 Save the program file in a "workers" directory, then run the program to see the worker pool results

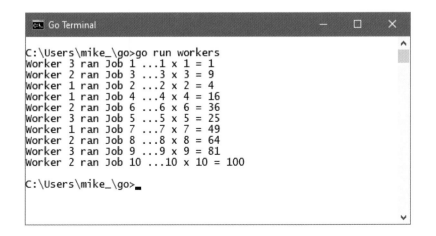

```
C:\Users\mike_\go>go run workers
Worker 3 ran Job 1 ...1 x 1 = 1
Worker 2 ran Job 3 ...3 x 3 = 9
Worker 1 ran Job 2 ...2 x 2 = 4
Worker 1 ran Job 4 ...4 x 4 = 16
Worker 2 ran Job 6 ...6 x 6 = 36
Worker 3 ran Job 5 ...5 x 5 = 25
Worker 1 ran Job 7 ...7 x 7 = 49
Worker 2 ran Job 8 ...8 x 8 = 64
Worker 3 ran Job 9 ...9 x 9 = 81
Worker 2 ran Job 10 ...10 x 10 = 100

C:\Users\mike_\go>
```

Hot tip

"Worker Pools" are also known as "Thread Pools". They can result in better performance as they don't need to create a new thread for each task.

Summary

- Parallelism is when two tasks are performed simultaneously.

- Concurrency is the separation of program code into separate tasks that could potentially be performed simultaneously.

- Goroutines provide the ability for lines of code to be executed concurrently.

- A goroutine is created by inserting the **go** keyword before an ordinary function call or method call.

- The Go standard library **sync** package provides a **WaitGroup** type that can wait for multiple goroutines to finish.

- A **WaitGroup** has an **Add( )** incrementing method, a **Done( )** decrementing method, and a **Wait( )** blocking method.

- When passing a **WaitGroup** as an argument to a function, it must be passed as a pointer.

- A Go channel is like a pipe through which the program can send and receive messages.

- A channel is created by specifying the **chan** keyword and a data type as arguments to the built-in **make( )** function.

- Deadlock is a fatal error where the program cannot proceed.

- The built-in **close( )** function can explicitly close a channel.

- Adding a buffer size argument to the **make( )** function enables multiple items to be sent as a queue to a channel.

- A **select** statement block can be used to simultaneously listen for messages from multiple channels.

- Enclosing a **select** statement block within an infinite **for** loop allows a program to continuously listen for channel messages.

- Channels can connect goroutines in a pipeline that sends and receives messages to synchronize the goroutines.

- The **<-** arrow operator can be used in function parameters to specify whether channels may only send or only receive.

- A worker pool can send tasks from multiple concurrent calls to a goroutine for completion in a random order set.

12 Request Responses

Listen for Requests

The Go standard library **net** package contains an **http** package that provides utilities that make it easy to create a web server. These utilities can be made available to your program by importing the **net/http** package.

The **http.ListenAndServe( )** function enables the program to start a web server running. It requires two arguments to specify a TCP network address string and a request handler. The address string specifies a port number to which the web server should listen for incoming requests. The port number must be prefixed by a : colon character within the string – for example, **":8000"** to listen for incoming requests on local port 8000. The default handler is typically used by specifying a **nil** second argument.

The **http.ListenAndServe( )** function always returns a non-nil error, and blocks forever. This means that lines of code below the call to this function will never be executed. The web server will continue to listen for incoming requests until the program gets terminated.

src\server\main.go

1. Begin by importing the Go standard library **net/http** package into a program
```
import (
    "fmt"
    "net/http"
)
```

2. Next, add a main function that will output a startup message and start a web server listening to local port 8000 on your system
```
func main( ) {

    // Statements to be inserted here later.

    fmt.Println( "Starting web server on port 8000" )
    http.ListenAndServe( ":8000", nil )

}
```

3. Save the program file in a "server" directory, then run the program to start the web server

Hot tip

Local system addresses are referenced via the loopback network http interface using the hostname **localhost**. This normally resolves to the IP address **127.0.0.1**.

...cont'd

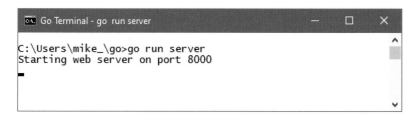

Don't forget

You can hit **Ctrl + C** to terminate a running program.

4 If a firewall security warning appears, confirm that you wish to allow access for the web server

5 Now, launch a web browser and visit **localhost:8000** to see the web server reply with a default message

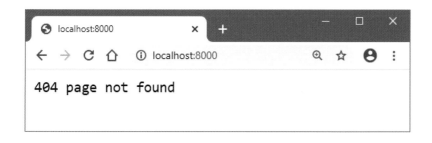

Hot tip

The web server does not yet know how to respond, but this chapter will develop the program to enable responses.

Handle a Request

In order for a Go web server to handle incoming requests, the program needs to register "route handlers" that specify how to respond to particular requests.

The **net/http** package provides an **http.HandleFunc( )** function that will register a route handler. This function requires two arguments to specify a string pattern describing the path to listen for, and the name of the function that will be called to provide a response when the specified path is recognized. The string pattern will begin with a / forward slash character – for example, **"/hello"**. This specifies that the web server should listen for incoming requests in our example from **localhost:8000/hello**.

A request handler function will, by default, always have parameters for an **http.ResponseWriter** object, to write a response to the request, and a pointer to an **http.Request** object containing information about the request – for example, its **URL.Path** contains the string pattern specified to the **http.HandleFunc( )** function. Typically, the **http.ResponseWriter** object is simply given the name **w**, and the **http.Request** object pointer is given the name **r**.

The **http.ResponseWriter** object has a **Write( )** method that accepts a **byte** slice argument of characters to be sent in a response. The characters can be converted into a string, like this:

w.Write([ ]byte(*"response string"*))

It is, however, more convenient to pass a string to the **http.ResponseWriter** object using a **WriteString( )** function contained in the Go standard library **io** (input/output) package. This can be made available by importing the **io** package.

The **io.WriteString( )** function requires two arguments to specify the **http.ResponseWriter** object, and the string to be sent in response to a request.

1. Begin by adding the instruction to import the Go standard library **io** package into the previous program
```
import (
    "fmt"
    "io"
    "net/http"
)
```

src\server\main.go
(continued)

2 Next, at the start of the main function, insert a statement to register a route handler
http.HandleFunc("/hello", helloHandler)

3 Now, after the main function, add the handler function that will write two strings as a request response
func helloHandler(w http.ResponseWriter, r *http.Request) {

　　　io.WriteString(w, "Response from the helloHandler!\n")
　　　io.WriteString(w, "URL.Path = " + r.URL.Path)
}

4 Save the updated program file in the "server" directory, then run the program to start the web server

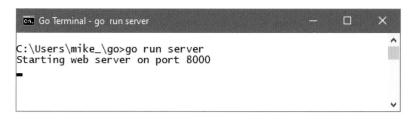

5 If a firewall security warning appears, confirm that you wish to allow access for the web server

6 Launch a web browser and visit **localhost:8000/hello** to see the web server respond to this request

Add Files to Serve

Having established that the server program can respond to requests with the example on page 177, files can be added to the program that the server can deliver in response to requests.

Web server files are typically contained within a root directory named **htdocs** (hypertext documents) or a similar name. This will generally contain HTML files and perhaps a **favicon.ico** image to identify the website in the browser's title bar. The root directory will also often contain sub-directories to group associated files – such as images in an **img** folder, style sheets in a **css** folder, etc.

In our server example, two HTML documents have been added to a root **htdocs** directory alongside a **favicon.ico** image. A single style sheet resides within an **htdocs/css** directory, and several images are contained in an **htdocs/img** directory. The entire server program tree now looks like this:

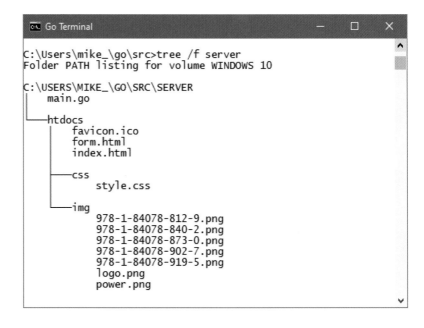

```
C:\Users\mike_\go\src>tree /f server
Folder PATH listing for volume WINDOWS 10

C:\USERS\MIKE_\GO\SRC\SERVER
    main.go
    htdocs
        favicon.ico
        form.html
        index.html
        css
            style.css
        img
            978-1-84078-812-9.png
            978-1-84078-840-2.png
            978-1-84078-873-0.png
            978-1-84078-902-7.png
            978-1-84078-919-5.png
            logo.png
            power.png
```

favicon.ico
32px x 32px

power.png 100px x 25px

Several of the image files are cover shots of various books whose ISBN (International Standard Book Number) is used as the respective cover image file name. The **img** directory also contains a company logo image, and a label to identify the web server.

...cont'd

The style sheet contains rules to specify the appearance of a web page response that will be written dynamically by the program:

style.css

```
img, p   { float: left }
p        { width: 320px ; text-align: center ; font-size: 1.5em }
```

The HTML document named **index.html** is a simple static web page displaying the website icon, a page heading and a label:

index.html

```
<!DOCTYPE HTML>
<html lang="en">
<head>
  <meta charset="UTF-8">
  <title>Index</title>
  <link rel="shortcut icon" href="favicon.ico">
</head>
  <body>
   <h1>Static Web Page</h1>
   <img src="img/power.png" alt="Power">
  </body>
</html>
```

179

The HTML document named **form.html** allows the user to submit a single text value to the web server:

form.html

```
<!DOCTYPE HTML>
<html lang="en">
<head>
  <meta charset="UTF-8">
  <title>Submission Form</title>
  <link rel="shortcut icon" href="favicon.ico">
</head>
<body>
<fieldset>
<legend>Book Lookup</legend>
  <form method="POST" action="lookup">
    <label>Programming Language</label>
    <input name="Language" type="text" value="">
    <input type="submit" value="Submit" >
  </form>
  </fieldset>
<img src="img/power.png" alt="Power">
</body>
</html>
```

Hot tip

The **POST** method will be tested by the server; the **lookup** value will identify a form handler function; and the **Language** value will identify the submitted value.

Deliver a Static Page

The Go standard library **net/http** package provides three functions that allow a web server to easily respond to all HTTP requests with the contents of a nominated file system.

The path of the root file directory is first specified as the argument to an **http.Dir( )** function. This returns a **Dir** type that is then specified as the argument to an **http.FileServer( )** function. This, in turn, returns a handler to respond to all HTTP requests with contents from the nominated root file directory.

Finally, an **http.Handle( )** function is used to register the handler. This requires two arguments to specify a route pattern and the handler's name. Typically, the pattern "/" is used as the first argument – to match all request paths.

The web browser can now request any document by name from within the nominated root file directory. If the file name is omitted from the request, the server will automatically seek a document named **index.html** to deliver to the browser.

src\server\main.go
(continued)

1 At the start of the main function, insert a statement to nominate the root directory of files to serve
dir := http.Dir("C:/Users/mike_/go/src/server/htdocs")

2 Next, create a request handler for that file system
fileServer := http.FileServer(dir)

3 Now, register the handler for all HTTP requests
http.Handle("/", fileServer)

4 Save the updated program file, then start the web server and visit **localhost:8000/index.html** (or simply visit **localhost:8000**) to see a static index web page

Don't forget

You will need to edit the path to the root file directory to its location on your own system.

Log Received Data

Having successfully delivered a static index web page, the program can now supply a form page for the submission of data.

The **http.Request** object has a **ParseForm( )** method that populates an **http.Request.Form** object with submitted form input values. A submitted value can then be retrieved by specifying the form input name as an argument to an **http.Request.FormValue( )** method.

There is also an **http.Request.Method** object containing the value assigned to the form's HTML **method** attribute. The "POST" method is preferred for the submission of form data.

If a form submission cannot be parsed, or if the form is using the wrong submission method, an error message can be sent to the browser by the **http.Error( )** function. This requires three arguments to specify the **http.ResponseWriter** name, an error string message, and an HTTP status code – such as **400** (bad request) or **405** (method not allowed).

Go provides constants for each HTTP status code, such as 200 with **http.StatusOk**. See the documentation at golang.org/pkg/net/http for the full list of codes.

Submitted form values can be formatted using the Go standard library **strings** package to trim spaces and change case. These values can then be written into a log file created using the **OpenFile( )** function in the Go **os** package. The Go standard library **log** package provides a **SetOutput( )** function, to specify the log file to write to, and a **Print( )** function to specify what should be written into the log file. This usefully prefixes each item logged with the date and time of writing.

1 Begin by adding instructions to import the Go standard library **strings**, **os**, and **log** packages into the previous program
```
import (
    "fmt"
    "io"
    "log"
    "net/http"
    "os"
    "strings"
)
```

src\server\main.go
(continued)

2 Next, in the main function, register a form handler with a route argument that will recognize the name assigned to the form's HTML **action** attribute
```
http.HandleFunc( "/lookup", formHandler )
```

src\server\main.go
(continued)

Hot tip

The most used request methods are **GET** and **POST**. The **GET** method appends data to the URL string. The **POST** method carries data in the request body, so is more secure and is the preferred method when transferring data from a browser to the server.

...cont'd

3 After the main function, begin the form handler with validation that checks the submission method assigned to the form's **method** attribute

```
func formHandler( w http.ResponseWriter, r *http.Request )
{
    if r.Method != "POST" {
        http.Error( w, "Method Not Allowed", 405 )
        return
    }

    // Statements to be inserted here.
}
```

4 Next, in the form handler, insert statements to parse the form data or return an error message to the browser

```
err := r.ParseForm( )
if err != nil {
    http.Error( w, "Bad Request", 400 )
    return
}
```

5 Now, in the form handler, insert statements to format a submitted value by removing spaces and changing case

```
lang := r.FormValue( "Language" )
lang = strings.ToLower( strings.Trim( lang, " " ) )
```

6 Then, in the form handler, insert statements to write the formatted value into a log file

```
file, err := os.OpenFile( "htdocs/data.log",
        os.O_CREATE|os.O_APPEND|os.O_WRONLY, 0644 )
if err != nil {
    log.Print( err )
}
defer file.Close( )
log.SetOutput( file )
log.Print( lang )
```

7 Save the updated program file, then start the web server and visit **localhost:8000/form.html** to see the form appear

8 Enter the name of a programming language in the input field, then hit the **Submit** button to submit the form data

For simplicity, this example submits only one item, which is referenced using the request object's **FormValue( )** method and HTML **name** attribute value. For forms that submit multiple items, you can loop through them using the **range** keyword to reference the key (HTML **name** attribute) and value (HTML **value** attribute) of each item.

9 Now, hit the browser's **Back** button and repeat the submission process to send multiple requests – each for a different programming language

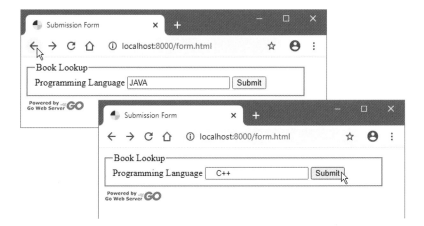

10 Then, visit **localhost:8000/data.log** to see each one of the submitted form values in the log file

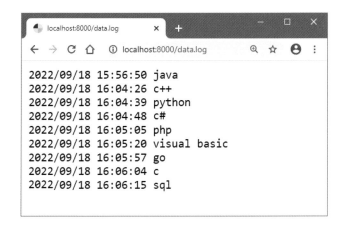

LOG

data.log

Deliver a Dynamic Response

Having received and logged the request data, following the steps on page 182-3, the program can now evaluate the request and send an appropriate response to the web browser.

src\server\main.go
(continued)

1 After the log statements in the form handler, initialize two variables with default response string values

```
title := "<a href='http://www.ineasysteps.com'>
                             See all titles online</a>"

isbn := "logo"
```

2 Next, examine the submitted request value and, if matched, assign appropriate response values

```
switch lang {
    case "c" :
        title = "C Programming"
        isbn = "978-1-84078-840-2"
    case "go" :
        title = "Go Programming"
        isbn = "978-1-84078-919-5"
    case "java" :
        title = "Java"
        isbn = "978-1-84078-873-0"
    case "python" :
        title = "Python"
        isbn = "978-1-84078-812-9"
    case "sql" :
        title = "SQL"
        isbn = "978-1-84078-902-7"
}
```

Hot tip

Notice that single quotes are used inside the string to distinguish between the outer double quotes, and so avoid prematurely terminating the string.

3 Now, build an HTML string that incorporates the response values

```
response :=
"<!DOCTYPE HTML><title>Web Server Response</title>"
response +=
        "<link rel='shortcut icon' href='favicon.ico'>"
response +=
        "<link rel='stylesheet' href='css/style.css'>"
response += "<p>" + title + "<br>in easy steps"
if isbn != "logo" {
        response += "<br>ISBN:" + isbn
}
response +=
"</p><img src='img/" + isbn + ".png' alt='Cover'>"
response += "<img src='img/power.png' alt='Power'>"
```

...cont'd

4 Finally, add a statement to send the response
io.WriteString(w, response)

5 Save the updated program file once more and start the web server, then visit **localhost:8000/form.html** to send requests and receive responses

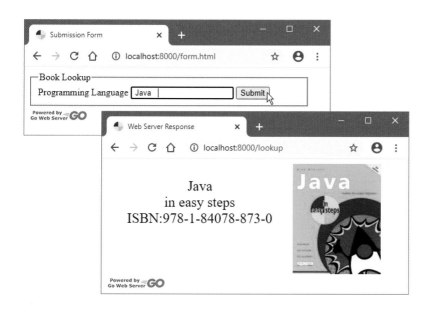

185

Hot tip

You can discover many more programming language books in this series – including R for Data Analysis in easy steps that covers the R programming language – at **www.ineasysteps.com**

Summary

- The Go standard library **net/http** package provides utilities to create a web server.

- The **http.ListenAndServe( )** function specifies an address at which to listen, and the name of a request handler.

- A web server program must register route handlers that specify how to respond to particular requests.

- The **http.HandleFunc( )** function specifies a route to listen for, and the name of a function that will handle that request.

- A request handler function signature always has parameters for an **http.ResponseWriter** object and an **http.Request** object.

- An **http.ResponseWriter** object has a **Write( )** method that can accept a **[ ]byte** slice to send in a response.

- The **io** package provides a **WriteString( )** function that can pass a **string** to an **http.ResponseWriter** object for a response.

- Files can be added to a web server program to be delivered to the browser in response to its requests.

- The **http.Dir( )** function nominates a root file system path.

- The **http.FileServer( )** function returns a handler for the contents of the file system specified as its argument.

- The **http.Handle( )** function specifies a route and the name of a handler for requests made to the nominated file system.

- The **http.Request.ParseForm( )** method populates an **http.Request.Form** object with submitted form data.

- The **http.Request.Method** object contains the value assigned to the HTML form's method attribute.

- The **http.Error( )** function can use an **http.ResponseWriter** object to send an error message and status to the browser.

- The Go standard library **log** package has **SetOutput( )** and **Print( )** functions to write time-stamped items to a log file.

- A web server program can build an HTML string to send a dynamic response to the web browser.

Index

M

N

O

P

Q

R

S

T

U

V

X

Z